# Ayya's

## A C C O U N T S

# Ayya's
## ACCOUNTS

# A LEDGER OF HOPE IN
# MODERN INDIA

**ANAND PANDIAN** & **M. P. MARIAPPAN**
*Afterword by Veena Das*

INDIANA UNIVERSITY PRESS
Bloomington and Indianapolis

*This book is a publication of*

Indiana University Press
Office of Scholarly Publishing
Herman B Wells Library 350
1320 East 10th Street
Bloomington, Indiana 47405 USA

iupress.indiana.edu

*Telephone*  800-842-6796
*Fax*        812-855-7931

⊖ The paper used in this publication
meets the minimum requirements of
the American National Standard for
Information Sciences—Permanence
of Paper for Printed Library Materials,
ANSI Z39.48–1992.

*Manufactured in the
United States of America*

*Library of Congress
Cataloging-in-Publication Data*

Pandian, Anand.
  [Micham meethi. English]
  Ayya's accounts : a ledger of hope in
modern India / Anand Pandian and
M.P. Mariappan ; afterword by
Veena Das.
    pages cm
  Includes bibliographical references.
  ISBN 978-0-253-01258-6 (hardback) —
  ISBN 978-0-253-01250-0 (paperback) —
  ISBN 978-0-253-01266-1 (e-book)
  1. Mariappan, M. P., 1919– 2. Tamil
(Indic people)—India—Biography.
3. Tamil (Indic people)—India—Social
conditions—20th century. 4. Nadars—
Biography. 5. Nadars—Social conditions
—20th century. 6. India—Social con-
ditions—20th century. 7. Merchants—
India—Biography. I. Mariappan, M. P.,
1919– II. Das, Veena. III. Title.
  DS489.25.T3P35813 2014
  954'.82—dc23
  [B]

                            2013042011

1 2 3 4 5 19 18 17 16 15 14

*For Karun and Uma,*
*for their cousins, and for*
*the others yet to come*

A couplet like a mustard seed, pierced and filled
with the seven seas . . .

*—Attributed to the medieval Tamil poet*
*and mystic Idaikkadar*

# CONTENTS

# CONTENTS

# PREFACE

This book grows out of conversations with my grandfather. I was born and raised in the United States. He has spent most of his life in India and Burma. The chapters pass back and forth between my voice and his, between his recollections of his life as a merchant and my reflections on his life as a grandson and an anthropologist. Although my grandfather has long had many languages within reach—some Hindi, Telugu, Burmese, English— the two of us have always spoken in Tamil, his native language.

Tamil is a diglossic language, with tremendous differences of feeling, implication, and solemnity between its written and spoken registers. My grandfather has always been a man of plain words and sparing expressions, a thrifty merchant with little interest in ornamentation of any kind. Nevertheless, there is a stark beauty to his stories.

In the original Tamil edition of this book, published by Kalachuvadu Publications in 2012, we sought to convey the modest elegance of my grandfather's language by relying on his own verbal idioms and the spoken quality of his vernacular Madurai dialect. With this English edition, based on my translation of his words, I have tried to maintain some sense of the colloquial personality of his speech.

What I know of Tamil was learned in bits and pieces over many years. "Every word in Tamil has ever so many meanings," my grandfather has often said to me. With this translation, I have tried to keep this idea in mind, working out the various meanings and implications that a single word may bear in diverse circumstances, while also striving, at the same time, to relay something of the simple clarity of my grandfather's voice.

What I mean to say is this: the person speaking here about his own life is not exactly him. Nor am I still the one who began, some time ago, to listen closely to his words. This is what happens when you do anthropology. In fact, this is what happens whenever you really listen to someone else. Your experience is no longer your own.

*Anand Pandian*
*Baltimore, Md.*
*November 2013*

*Note: This symbol,* ～, marks each passage between Ayya's voice and mine.

# Ayya's

## ACCOUNTS

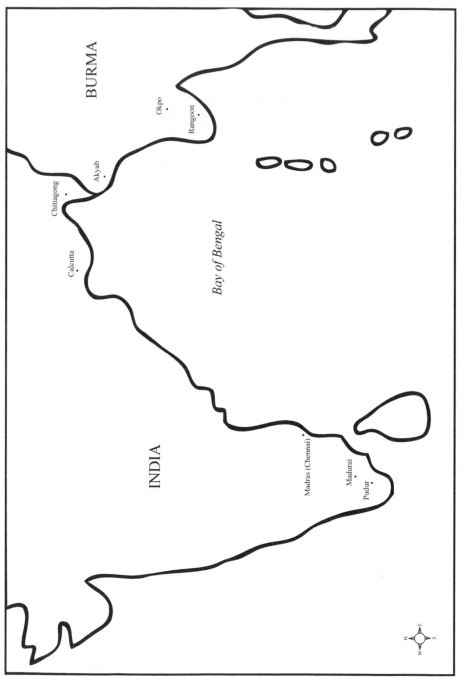

India and Burma, 1941

# A CENTURY OF EXPERIENCE

1

We were on a train clattering to Madurai seventeen years ago when my grand-father first told me the story of his passage back from Burma to India in 1941. Ayya had come of age in a small town in the lush lowlands north of Rangoon. For nearly a decade, he and his brothers kept a shop there, on the veranda of their house. Then the Second World War reached their town, driving them back to India. One among hundreds of thousands of refugees,

Ayya survived a deadly trek through the bamboo jungles of western Burma and landed in the dry, dusty village of his forebears in southern Tamil Nadu. He married, and with patience, thrift, luck, and cunning, he eventually secured a decent life for his family.

I sat beside Ayya on a green vinyl berth as he described all of this, grateful for the cool, dry air of this coach car on the Pandyan Express. It was early June. The unrelenting heat outside was thick, sticky. But there was something else that I could almost feel floating in the air around my grandfather: the absence of Paati, my grandmother.[1] It had been just four months since Ayya had lost his wife. And now it seemed, as he spoke, that this loss was cloaked in other losses that he'd seen—the mother who had died when he was a child, the father he'd buried back in Burma, the rubble of their livelihood there. "Who was left to tell me stories?" he asked plaintively, as if, for a moment, the septuagenarian widower was once again that orphaned child.

I also missed my grandmother and the raucous tales that she could tell. I'd grown up in New York and Los Angeles. Every year or two, we would see Ayya and Paati for a few weeks at a time. I don't remember Ayya being a very avid or captivating storyteller in those years. In fact, he was rather quiet. Most of what I knew about him came from the stories that others would tell about his life: his ceaseless toils, the hardships he had survived, and the responsibility that all of us had inherited to struggle in turn. Ayya was never one to call attention to himself. But at a certain moment late in life, perhaps when he began to feel the tremors of his own mortality, my grandfather found that he had a lot to tell. And I happened to be there to listen.

This was something that began as an accident, my presence beside my grandfather as he reflected on his life. But then, over time, listening to him became more of a habit. For most of his years, he had made a living by dealing in fruit. As his eldest grandson, and an anthropologist, I learned to make my living by dealing in the stories of others like him. I began to travel often from the United States to India, spending many years with farmers, activists, writers, and filmmakers in the south Indian state of Tamil Nadu, where my grandfather lived. On these many trips, I would always pass in and out of Ayya's company. And slowly, I began to see how deeply my pursuit of this vocation had been shaped by my sense of his history.

Most of us have had grandparents or other elders murmuring from the corners of our lives, sharing tales that are sometimes riveting, sometimes simply tedious. The lessons of their experience may go heeded or unheeded by those who follow them. But with Ayya, I found that I couldn't shake the sense of a deep and insistent debt.

Something about this debt was very personal. My grandfather's life had taken a precarious route, nothing like the stiff railroad tracks that led us to Madurai that night or the steady beat of our passage over them. What if his journey had suddenly ground to an unexpected halt? What would I have become, if anything at all?

But there was also something else that I began to see by listening to my grandfather, a lesson in the formidable reach of historical perspective. There he was, a small man seated beside me in a musty railway compartment, passing the time with stories that stretched far beyond the south Indian countryside we were traversing, chronicling events that I could barely recall from the pages of my American school textbooks. Where on his person could he have kept this immensity, this vast world of his experience?

No life is as small as it might first appear from a distance. Extraordinary tales may be found in the most unlikely places. This book grows out of a simple faith—the idea that you can tell the story of a place as large and complex as modern India through the life of a single individual, through the life of someone like my grandfather, Ayya.

The year is 2014. Nearly a century has passed since Ayya's birth in 1919. He has sipped water from open wells, roadside gullies, plastic bottles, and pots of yesterday's rice. He's been spurned in rural India for belonging to a despised caste of tree climbers and celebrated in New York City for being the father of an Indian physician. He has grandchildren who teach in elementary schools, design telecommunications hardware, and exhibit artworks all over Europe. He's mistaken airplanes for vultures, run from Japanese bombers, sent a son to the Indian Air Force, and flown between Chennai and Los Angeles at least ten times. He has survived the plague and prostate cancer. He's traded in paper, saris, matchboxes, limes, and pomegranates. He has lost a daughter under mysterious circumstances, seen many things that he never dreamed were possible, and quietly buried countless wishes unknown to anyone else.

What could the peculiar quirks of such a life tell us about modern India? What does such experience have to do with India now? Everyone knows that many things in India are changing very quickly. We see books about *India Becoming,* documentaries on an *India Rising,* political slogans that seek to celebrate an "India Shining." Everything seems to be happening at once, as though a slumbering giant has finally awakened.

This image, of a stirring behemoth, is a familiar one. This is something that we have been told for a long time: that India is an old land, that India has long refused to change, that only now has India finally arrived at the threshold of something radically new, radically different. There are good reasons, however, to distrust such a story.

Think back to a century ago, 1913: how much of that India would be recognizable now? King George V of England was the emperor of India. Mohandas K. Gandhi hadn't yet returned to India from distant Natal, South Africa, where he was working with Indian coal miners and railway laborers. There were nearly 200,000 acres of land sown with opium in India, much of which was meant for official export to China. Lines extending for 2,725 miles conveyed fewer than 4 million words that year through the chief means of long-distance communication, the telegraph. There were about 10,000 men and fewer than 300 women enrolled in the colleges and universities of the Madras Presidency in southern India. The town of Madurai had a recorded population of 134,130 individuals, less than one-tenth of what it numbers now a century later.

How to tell the story of what has happened since in India? The nationalist struggle for independence from Britain. The violence exercised in the name of social and religious solidarity. The forceful remaking of cities and the countryside in the name of development. The rise of a free-market economy and a consumer society. The emergence of vibrant diasporic communities overseas. These are massive currents of change, which can be surveyed from a distance for their patterns and directions. But there are other aspects of their texture that can be grasped only through a more intimate mode of inquiry.

Large places often have their stories told through the lives of exemplary individuals. Think of Gandhi, for example, widely portrayed as the very soul of India. Then there are those ways of imagining such places themselves in personal or biographical terms. Recall this famous description of India from Jawaharlal Nehru's 1946 *Discovery of India:*

Shameful and repellent she is occasionally, perverse and obstinate, sometimes even a little hysteric, this lady with a past. But she is very lovable
and none of her children can forget her wherever they go or whatever
strange fate befalls them. For she is part of them in her greatness as well
as her failings, and they are mirrored in those deep eyes of hers that have
seen so much of life's passion and joy and folly and looked down into
wisdom's well.

The rescue of a distressed damsel was no doubt on the mind of this impris-
oned nationalist leader, who would go on to serve as the first prime minister
of an independent India. Striking, however, are all the shades and nuances
that Nehru teases out of this portrait of an individual.

Such narratives make sense only because of the unity they attribute to the
experience of their subjects. Either implicitly or explicitly, these stories rely
upon the idea of an overarching trajectory, the movement of a wider arc of
possibility and defeat. The trajectory of modern India has been sketched in
various ways: as a journey into freedom, as a climb into prosperity, even as a
dark descent into chaos. Regardless of the direction that is assigned to India
by such stories, what we often find is an idealization of the course—like
those railway tracks, once again.

Most tales of modern India these days are epic accounts of victory and
defeat. There are the industrial titans who tug on our admirations and jeal-
ousies, and the anguished paupers who elicit sympathy and disdain. There
is no doubt something riveting in the trials and triumphs of exceptional figures. But perhaps there is also something to learn from those who have lived
between these poles, those who saw big things happen and caught just some
of their momentum, those who found modest success in a life of trouble,
chance, nerve, and ruse.

Here is the story of M. P. Mariappan, whose letters to Shillong, New
York, Lucknow, and Nashville were stamped for decades with a double-lined
oval that curved around his small place in the world:

Limes and Fruits Commission Agent
208-A North Masi St.
Madurai 625001
INDIA

It's a story about those parents, schoolchildren, shopkeepers, and refugees whose interwoven fates make up the landscape of contemporary India. It's also a story about all the rest of us who found our own way along the paths they laid.

Here he is now, seated on a rickety wooden bench, getting ready for his morning walk. We're in the foyer of a modest, sandy brown bungalow in Anna Nagar, Madurai, built in 1983.[2] Ayya is wearing black shorts and an old blue T-shirt. He's mostly bald, except for wispy tufts of white above his eyes and behind his head, and the thick curls of hair on his arms. He looks small and stout as he pulls on a pair of loose white socks, which bunch up below his thin calves. These sagging socks speak to his lifelong habits of thrift, while the scar on his forehead still marks a childhood accident nearly ninety years back. A century of history, a century of experience, all remaining with him still, lingering in every space and moment of his life.

Carefully stepping into a well-worn pair of black walking shoes, the rubber grip of his walking stick in hand, Ayya leaves the house. A tin board hung from the metal grillwork outside details, somewhat mysteriously, the qualifications of a man who moved to New York City in 1972: Dr. M. Ganesa Pandian, MD, FRCP (Canada) (Cardiology), AB (USA), FACA—my father, his firstborn child, living in America like half of Ayya's children and most of his grandchildren, like the families of so many others in this middle-class urban neighborhood.

Striding over the fresh white *kolam* pattern that my aunt has applied to the ground in the gathering light of dawn, Ayya steps beyond the rusty gate of the courtyard. For the next hour, he will slowly trace and retrace a route through the smaller lanes of Anna Nagar. The morning begins quietly but builds quickly to a din of bustling traffic as children are rushed by bicycle, car, scooter, and auto rickshaw to a nearby school. He must be careful about these vehicles and the many potholes in the roads, but also about the traps that his own mind may set. Memories come as sudden distractions, making it difficult to see such dangers along his path.

Madurai is widely known as a temple city, the massive Meenakshi Amman temple complex across the river drawing pilgrims and tourists from all over India and around the globe. But Anna Nagar tells more about the city as a regional commercial capital, a bustling market for licit and illicit goods alike. Settled in its lanes are jewelers, lawyers, developers, doctors, and other merchants like Ayya. Many of their houses are built like fortresses, their gleaming faces of steel, glass, and cement towering coldly over the leafy roads of the neighborhood.

Beside these places, Ayya's house looks dated, weathered, even a bit rundown. But he's always been frugal with money, especially when it comes to ornamental niceties. Back at home after his walk, he has his breakfast at a peeling blue Formica table in the kitchen. He spends the rest of the morning in a padded black armchair in the living room, paging through the morning paper. Watching after him is my grandmother, Paati, looking down from a large, gold-painted frame hung high upon the wall. Between her steady gaze and the stream of events recorded in the newspaper, public and private life come together in this room.

A voice calls at the door, and the washerman interrupts his reading. Ayya is eager to tally up all the goods that the man has brought back. Sheets, pillowcases, towels, and shirts are each divided into individual piles and then added up. Ayya's slippered foot taps quietly in his chair as the dhobi calls out these numbers, 1, 2, 3, 4, 5 . . . It's as if the beat of the count lives within his own body, an unconscious rhythm of goods accumulating one by one. There is a pillowcase missing this morning, and Ayya feigns anger. Then he laughs and pays the man what is due. He looks for some old film songs on the television before lying down for a rest.

Ayya sleeps lightly and uneasily. There are too many memories, images, thoughts, and questions clamoring for attention behind his closed eyes. He was never one to keep journals, diaries, or other such reflections on the events of his life. He maintained ledgers of his business transactions and committed everything else to memory, consciously recalling the details of each day so often that he needed no written reminders. These habits pursue him now, even as he sleeps. He dreams of fruit brokers, unpaid debts, and truckloads of limes tallied one by one.

Look at some of the things scattered around Ayya as he rests: photographs of grandchildren dispersed throughout India and America; an image of the Shwedagon Pagoda's golden spire rising over Rangoon; a framed portrait of the "Grandfather of the Year" beaming with a plump Hawaiian pineapple in 1990; a magnet clinging to the steel green face of a bureau, showing a mouse, dog, and two cats playing jazz around a piano.

Bits of paper, plastic, and metal, fragile tokens of testimony and reminiscence, but also elements with which to conjure the wonder of an ordinary life in extraordinary times. Vast worlds lie buried within the smallest details of such a life.

Whenever we meet, there's something that Ayya always does. He reaches out with both of his hands to clasp my arms, just below my shoulders. I can feel his fingertips, pressing strongly into the slender bands of muscle, as if they're testing the resistance that they meet there, measuring the strength gathered around my bones.

Sometimes, a faint pulse of worry flickers through my mind, as I wonder whether he's judged me too weak. But if he's ever felt anything like this, it never shows in his eyes, which are always warm as he looks up and smiles.

His hands remain wrapped around my arms. His elbows are locked to fix a space between us. The seconds tick by. It feels like I'm some fond thing finally back in his hands, something whose condition can only be assessed slowly, and from the right kind of distance. A lifelong Indian trader, appraising his American grandson.

But let me admit this too—after some years of thinking and working as an anthropologist, I am also appraising him. My habits of appraisal depend, perhaps, on a different kind of distance, one that matches up what the person before me says and does with things that others like him have said and done. He's never just my grandfather. There's always some larger picture of human possibility that I tend to look for, composed of others I've met, others I've read about.

I know this kind of thinking is dangerous. You can lose sight of that person standing right there before you. This kind of thinking has to be done with care.

Early in 2012, I flew from Baltimore to Madurai to spend a few days with Ayya. *Adi!* he said, again and again, asking me to hit his own arms as hard as I could, to feel for myself how firm they still were. I did as he said, but quite gingerly and anxiously. Everyone was worried about him. He hadn't been able to eat lately, and when he walked, my aunt reported, he was leaning heavily over his walking stick for support.

I had traveled from America just to work with him on this book project, to go over notes, drafts, transcripts, and pending doubts and questions I still had about his life. But half the space in my bag was taken up with things meant simply to preserve this life: a giant bag of Raisin Bran, a bottle of moisturizing cream for cracking skin, a tub of sugarless Citrucel powder to aid his digestion. A sense of dread pooled in my stomach as I waited for the plane to take off.

When I got to Madurai, though, this feeling quickly passed. For Ayya, life went on. I could see that there was a thread carrying each moment of his life over into the next, act to act, conversation to conversation. It was no more than a feeling, the feeling of momentum that we sometimes call hope. Hope is something very small, so quiet and subtle, and yet it seemed, for Ayya, to make all the difference. There was always something more to live for.

In the last few years, this book project has also found a small place in Ayya's life. It began in bits and pieces scattered over the course of many years, dialogues we had here and there in the various places where our lives intersected: Chennai and Bangalore, Oakland and Los Angeles, even Burma where we went together in 2002 to look for his father's grave. It gained shape and momentum through the letters, phone calls, and ideas we exchanged in between these meetings. Slowly, as both of us grew older, it began to feel like a book that ought to be written.

Every life is infinite, composed by endless connections, cuts, and branches. No book can aspire to reach so deeply into anyone's experience. What you see here grows only from the questions that I've posed to Ayya over these last seventeen years, the things he's said in return, and the curiosity that we've shared for those fleeting moments in which our lives intertwined. "I've got a thousand and eight stories," Ayya sometimes says. This book is formed only from what I've remembered to ask him and what he's remembered to say.

All of us come to life in a sea of stories. They sketch what we desire and fear. They take us back to times and places we thought were gone and to others that we've never imagined. Woven from the many threads of our experience, they form patterns we didn't expect to see, directions we didn't expect to follow.

Stories are fragile and ephemeral things, shadowed always by the disappearance of their tellers and the fleeting circumstances of their birth. We may indeed be living these days in a world of blinding speed and startling pulse. Still, we need stories to make sense of this world and to judge how best to live with its challenges and possibilities.

Some time ago, Ayya began to joke about me as his computer, for all the things that I had been remembering and recording of his life. But I've begun to think of this book itself as another kind of recording device, more like the daily account books that Ayya always kept.

In those ledgers, each day is marked as a series of transactions, a list of things given and received. With every trade, expectations and returns accumulate, and their balance carries over to the day that follows. Day by day, page by page, something always remains, and it is with these remainders that Ayya has made a life for himself and for all those who followed him.

This book is also a kind of accounting. Its stories and lessons may be counted as debts and receipts. These debts and receipts ought, in principle, to fall into balance. But something always remains to be carried over, from one life into others yet to come.

The best word for that something, I think, is hope.

∾

# IN SOME VILLAGE, SOMEWHERE

# 2

*Each morning here in Madurai, I walk for an hour. And as I walk, I count. Say you were as old as me. Stumble over the bumps and dips in the road, and you'd probably fall to the ground like I would. So I hold on to my walking stick as I go. And as that stick keeps beating against the road, I count those beats to myself.*

*A hundred and ten beats from the house to the end of the road . . . from there to the rice mill, another forty . . . Dr. Bhaskar's house is three hundred beats away, and from there, until the end of the road, another three hundred beats . . .*

*This isn't something I do just to pass the time. There's a good reason that I count like this: I don't want to suddenly remember something else, somewhere else, in the life that I've lived. Count like this when you walk, and your thoughts won't drift to anything else.*

*Pay attention. Don't trip over a rock. Just keep counting as you walk. And those numbers, those steps—one, two, three—are all that you will see.*

*At night too, it's just like this. Sleep comes only if I count. And when I dream, those dreams will come in countless numbers.*

*Thoughts are dreams that come in countless numbers, they say. You can try to put a stop to them, but then there would be nothing left to live for. Our lives, people's lives, are nothing more than this: an endless stream of thoughts.*

Where I was born, when I was born, I have no idea. I have seven children, and each of them celebrates my birthday on a different day. One son wishes me on one day. Then comes another day, and some other daughter-in-law has birthday wishes. I don't remember any of these days. "Happy birthday, Ayya!" they say, but I just blink. No one's ever told me when I was born, or where I was born.

I would say that I was born in 1919, but this is only a guess. Back then, my father, Appa, had a small business in Burma.[1] Who went to Burma first? At what time? From what generation? You might have these questions, but I have no answers. I think I was probably born in Burma myself. But this is also a guess. If I was born there, my Amma must have also been there with him. Did Appa take her there after their marriage? Even this, I don't know.

Appa named me after my grandfather, Mariappan. Amma, though, would never say my name. Mariappan was also her father-in-law's name, and so, out of respect to him, she called me Ramasamy. I know that I was her fourth child. I had three elder brothers, and I knew two of them very well. I don't know anything at all about her third boy. He died a long time ago.

My grandmother, Appa's mother, belonged to the village of Pudur. For a long time, we lived in that small village, in my grandmother's house. My father would leave us behind in Pudur to study, and he would go off to Burma to look after his shop. He'd come back once every three months and stay up to a month each time, with his wife and children. Then he'd go back once more to look after his business.

Those days, they would make an astrological forecast for each child. Appa had this done for all of us. He kept the details of my birth locked up in an iron safe in Burma, where I lived with him later for many years. When the Second World War began, we suddenly had to come back to India. All that we had there, we left behind, locked up in the shop.

We left behind my astrological forecast too, along with everything else in that iron safe. "Some day I'll have to come back to Burma, and I'll get it then," I thought to myself. But I didn't go back again to Burma for sixty years. And when I finally did, there was nothing left to find.

Amma's name was Mookamma. Mookamma, Kathamma, those were the kinds of names they gave back then. Born with a big nose? They'd call you Mookamma. Born with big ears? They'd call you Kathamma.[2] Amma was from Vaduvarpatti, and her family was very poor. We would often go to their village, which was fifteen kilometers from Pudur. We knew that when we went to visit them, they would feed us well.

We had to go there on foot, and walk back as well. By the time we got back home, we would always be exhausted. Thirsty too. Suppose we stopped at a house in a village along the way, to ask for some water. At first they'd say that they couldn't give us any. "What's your caste?" they'd ask. "Ok, sit down and cup your hands," they'd say, and pour the water into our hands to drink. When you're so thirsty that you could die, you would do exactly as they said. This was what we experienced in those days.

There were those who were very wealthy back then, and those who were poor and suffering. But I knew nothing about how anyone else lived at the time. There were so many people with nothing to eat, people who'd come begging from house to house. "Amma, please, a little gruel . . . Amma, please, a little gruel . . ." they'd cup their hands and ask. There were people who were that poor back then, but we never needed to beg like that.

We never starved. There was always gruel at least to eat: a millet gruel, something like that. Pudur was a dry place where rice didn't grow, so only the rich ate rice. We had other grains, millets like *keppai, kambu, cholam, tinai*; this was what we ate. You had to pound the chaff away, grind the grains into flour, and make this into a paste to eat. All of this had to be done by hand. There was more than enough work for the women in the house.

We lived in a thatched hut at the time. The thatch was woven from palmyra and coconut fronds and the walls were made of mud. There was one room inside and verandas on either side. We always slept outside on those verandas because it was so stuffy inside. Whenever it rained, water would pour down through the thatch, and at night, when children needed to urinate, they'd squat where that rain came pouring down. We'd never go outside at night.

I never thought back then about whether this house was clean or comfortable. There were many kinds of houses in that village. Whenever I walked around, I could see that some people lived one way, and others lived some other way. Some had tiled houses; some had brick houses. Though I saw all these places, I didn't know to want such things for myself.

I had one piece of cloth to fasten around my waist, that was all. Even when I began to go to school, this was how I'd dress. I was already twelve years old when I got my first shirt to wear. I had joined the Boy Scouts in the sixth grade, and each of us got our own uniform shirts. I would wear mine only on days when we had our Scout drills. Otherwise, I'd wander around without a shirt. To be honest, it wasn't even a proper loincloth that I wore at the time. I had a string wrapped around my waist, onto which I would tie a bit of cloth.

Back then in Pudur, only the rich wore slippers on their feet. It was in Burma that I wore slippers for the first time. Even on that ship to Burma, eighty years back, I traveled barefoot.

I remember that as a boy, I really liked to play. We would look around in the garbage for some torn and useless cloth, which we'd wrap up into a round ball to throw around. In the game we used to play, you had to aim really carefully and try to hit the other boys with that ball. Wherever I was, wherever they were standing, I'd somehow manage to hit them on the back. It would always hit the mark, that ball. That's how well I used to play.

I was always very mischievous too. Wherever I went, I'd run off and run back without a thought. At school, they let us out on recess once each day. Whether we had to relieve ourselves, or find some water to drink, the school had nothing for us. We had to leave the school grounds to find something to drink. To relieve ourselves, we also had to go outside.

Recess would last for just ten minutes. All the boys would run and stand beside an old almond tree near the school. There were almonds lying all around that tree, and we'd quickly gather these up to eat— we had nothing like this at home. I remember that the flowers on that tree looked like coconut flowers; put one in your mouth, and it would taste a little sweet.

All the boys would race to grab those almonds, and I would also run with them. Once, when I was running like that, I suddenly tripped over a rock and fell, so fast that my head was badly hurt. There was blood dripping from my head, but I barely noticed what had happened. I didn't feel any pain, either. I just went back to the classroom, and when the teacher and the other boys looked at me, they were all shocked at what they saw.

"Look! This boy's gone and broken his head! There's blood everywhere," the teacher said. He took me and washed off the wound on my forehead. Back then, they used to try to stop the bleeding with country sugar made from sugarcane, mixed with a little lime powder. The teacher did this for me, then sent me back to the classroom once more.

Meanwhile, some boy had run home to tell Amma what had happened. "Mariappan's broke his head open!" he cried. "Look Amma, he'd ran off to gather some almonds, and then he went and broke his head like this."

Amma was very frightened. She was sobbing when she rushed to the school to find me. Then she saw me sitting down in the classroom, studying, and she began to calm down.

I studied in a Nadar school. There were people of all castes in that village: Brahmins, Pillais, Telugu Nayaks, Nadars, Chettiar weavers, Parayars, Chakkiliyar leatherworkers, and so on. All of them attended to their own trades and lived in their own areas. None of us were allowed into the Brahmin houses. They wouldn't give us water to drink, and if we gave them water, they wouldn't take it from us. They would wrap their hands in cloth to take their payments for temple services. People from untouchable castes couldn't even pass through the Brahmin street—they weren't allowed to wear shirts and slippers, even to carry umbrellas.

Each caste had its own customs. They were terrible, these arrangements. There was a Pillai man in that village, vegetarian by caste and custom. I remember once when his relatives had come back to Pudur from Burma. Appa had also come back at the same time, and that Pillai man put on a feast for all of them together. Appa took me along with him, but we were the only guests not allowed within that house. They laid out a banana leaf outside the house for Appa and me to eat from. We sat there on the veranda to eat, and then we came home. That caste wouldn't eat on a plate we ate on or drink from a cup we drank from; that's how it was back then.

Often, there were fights between different castes. The Nadars of the village came together to form an association, and they would meet once a month, collecting dues from each family: grain from farmers, cash from traders. They used these funds to build the school where I studied, the "Nadar Common School." It was finished in 1920 and managed by the Nadar community association. Children from all castes could study there, but Nadar children didn't have to pay any fees.

I was five years old when I first went to that school. We sat on a dirt floor and poked our fingers into that dirt to work out our sums. Then, when I was in the first grade, they gave us slates to study with. What they taught us first was the Tamil alphabet: a, aa, i, ii, and so on. Then there were Auvaiyar's *Athichudi* and *Konrai Vendhan* to learn, until the second or third grade.[3] We learned how to count with grains of rice.

Arithmetic and writing both came easily to me. I learned how to count in Tamil from 1, 2, 3 to 100, 1,000. Then we began to learn a little English in the third grade, and there were lessons in history, science, nature studies, and Tamil grammar. Though I enjoyed all of this, what I liked the most was arithmetic.

Even in those days, I could work very quickly with numbers. I mastered mathematics so well that the teacher would gape at my arithmetic. He would go to the chalkboard with a math question. We would have to stand up while we thought about it and stay on our feet as long as it took to work out the problem. Whoever knew the answer could sit down.

I would always sit down right away, while the other boys were still thinking. "How did you find the answer so soon, how did you work it out?" the teacher would come and ask me. I would explain what I did—"You do this, and then you do that, and then you do that . . ."

Sometimes, even he couldn't work out the answer right away. There he was, thinking to himself at the chalkboard, while I had figured it out and sat down right away. All the answers were printed at the back of his textbook. "You're right, boy," he'd say after looking back there. I always did well with mathematics. This was what I liked most of all at school.

There were about 120 children who studied at our school. We would all play together outside, boys and girls of many different castes. But in the classroom, the untouchable children alone were forbidden from sitting on the benches. Everyone else sat above them on the benches, but they had to sit on the ground below. They weren't given anything to eat at school, either. They had to eat whatever they'd brought with them, wrapped up in a bundle of cloth.

All this happened back when the British still ruled over India. Even in the schools, all the laws and rules were theirs. When to wake up each morning, what to do each evening, what time to go home each day . . . all of this happened according to their laws and rules. Every year, the school would get some funds from the government for its expenses, after an inspector came to examine what the students were being taught.

One year, they asked me to act in an English play. It was called *Albert, Our King.* I acted as the wife of a farmer. The farmer and his wife were out in a field, making chapatis. Albert and his soldiers were nearby, fighting with the ruler of another country. While they were fighting, the king went off by himself. He was hungry, and he wanted to satisfy his hunger. Then he saw this farmer and his wife.

"You wait," I said to him, as the farmer's wife. "Let me go get some more firewood. Then I'll make you some chapatis." The king had come here without telling any of his soldiers. He was worried about what would happen if they came to look for him. Then they saw him. "Hail hail, Albert our king!" they said. And he went back with his soldiers, without eating anything.

When the king left, this is what I said, in English: "King or no king, how could he leave without eating the chapatis!" And then everyone clapped, all those who had come to watch the play.

Each morning at school, there was a song that we had to sing in English:

God save our gracious king
Long live our noble king
God save our king
Send him victorious
Happy and glorious
Long to reign over us
God save the king

More than eighty years have passed, but I still remember each word of this song. I still know the tune, exactly as they taught us to sing it. Today, I can't remember where I walked this morning, but this song from so long ago, I remember it clearly. Unbelievable, isn't it?

∾

3

Ayya is surrounded by six of his children, most of his daughters-in-law, many of his grandchildren. We've come from Madurai, Chennai, Bangalore, Los Angeles, Sunnyvale, Columbus, Vancouver, a family dispersed through the Indo-Anglo-American world, a world brought into being by the colonial powers my grandfather was taught to venerate.

The hotel is opulent, catering to the expectations of overseas Indians. On the table are the remains of a lavish buffet. Ayya's fingers rest lightly on the edge of a half-eaten plate of yogurt rice. His cheeks are still scarred, darkened, by a recent battle with mouth cancer. He's learning how to eat once again, now that he can't wear his dentures at all.

What Ayya says without his teeth is sometimes difficult to understand. But when he does speak, everyone leans in quietly. His words about his struggles seem to give substance and presence to the story of his life. It's as though we can all see it, Ayya's story, as though it's something apart from him, something with a life of its own, lingering in the open space between us, wringing out feelings from each of these faces.

My grandfather knows that he's lucky to have so many looking after him. Many elderly in India lack such care. It was in a Tamil village not far from this hotel that I did my PhD research. There, I met old men and women who described themselves as cattle fit for slaughter. They complained of children chasing them out of houses—"Just get lost and die somewhere!" And there were rumors of pesticide tablets slipped into the curries of those who clung too stubbornly to life. There was even a name for this, I was told: *karunai kolai*, "mercy killing."

Ayya speaks of being satisfied with the little that he had as a child in the village of Pudur. But what could this mean for the children in this family now? So much has changed. Take the meat and vegetables left behind so casually on these plates, the thick braids of gold around the necks of the mothers, the fathers and their brand-name T-shirts from American department stores. India is known the world over for its ascetics, saints, and renunciants. What place do their philosophies of self-control have in a time of conspicuous indulgence?

There are other questions so remote that they barely arise. Suppose this hotel was as old as it looks. Eighty or ninety years ago, would we have even been permitted inside? The family is Nadar by caste—today, a prosperous community of merchants and professionals, but a century ago, reviled for its association with the country liquor produced from the palmyra palm. There's an old proverb that I've heard now and then: "The Parayar is polluting to touch, but even the sight of the Shanar is polluting." Hardly anyone remembers now that the Nadars were once maligned as unclean "Shanar" tree climbers, least of all the Nadars themselves.

Caste survives in India as a principle of social classification, one that begins with the simple question of whom one is allowed to marry. Gathered around Ayya that day, however, were many who had flouted this convention, men and women who had even married into communities that would have refused to eat from Nadar plates some time ago.

Me, for example. All of us were together at the Taj Malabar Hotel, in fact, because I had been married the day before in nearby Thrissur: my wife's father a Nair from Kerala, her mother a Tamil Pillai by caste.

That afternoon, I was sitting on the far side of the round wooden table. Tired, perhaps even bored, my thoughts kept drifting far from these details of my grandfather's life, these stories that I'd already heard so often.

Suddenly, Ayya said something that pulled me right back. Fixing his eyes in my direction, he asked me a question that felt more like a demand, something like a sharp reminder of a promise made long ago: "When are you going to write my history?"

I was startled and didn't know what to say. Ayya knew that I'd been working on a book based on my PhD research. Just yesterday, nearly a hundred villagers from my research area had come by bus to attend the wedding. Was Ayya hurt that I was writing about their lives instead of his own?

It's difficult to convey what happened next. Overwhelmed by a rush of conflicting feelings, I suddenly found it impossible to say what I had in mind. I remember blinking, beginning, stuttering, stopping. Blinking, stuttering, stopping again.

A puzzled silence settled around me. "Ayya," I finally managed to say, "it's always your history that I've been writing. With each person's story in that book, it's your story that I've been trying to write. Only by learning the story of your life did I come to see that people's lives have histories at all. Whatever I write, I write because of what I learned from you."

Something had been said, if not understood. The moment passed, but I remained uneasy. Did my grandfather believe what I'd just said? Did I? The questions kept pricking at me, whenever I came back to try to learn something more about India.

# THINGS I DIDN'T KNOW I'D LOST

# 4

AS A CHILD, I WAS VERY MISCHIEVOUS. AMMA NEVER SCOLDED US,
though; at least I don't remember her ever scolding me when I did
troublesome things.

When I was four or five years old, Appa bought us a milch cow,
and Amma was the one who milked it. She would boil some of
that milk and set it aside to make buttermilk. When it curdled, she
would draw out the buttermilk and churn the butter to make ghee.

If she left that ghee on the ground, flies and ants would come
swarming, so she would pour it into a mud pot and hang it up with
some rope from the roof of the house. I also liked ghee myself, but
she would hang it so high that I couldn't reach it. So this is what
I would do. I'd wait until she wasn't around and then drag over a
bench or something else to climb on. I would get that ghee and pour
it onto something to eat.

There were other pots also hanging from the roof, filled with
neem oil, castor oil, and sesame oil. Among these four or five pots,

there were at least two filled with something that looked like ghee. In the sunlight, they would also melt the same way. Sometimes, I'd take down one of those pots, thinking it was ghee, and mash it into what I was eating. "What's this, so bitter and terrible!" I remember saying to myself and dumping all of it off my plate. It must have been castor oil or something.

I'd always wait until Amma had left the house to try to eat that ghee—if she knew, she wouldn't let me touch it. "What's this, where's all the ghee? Maybe some cat or something came and ate it up?" she'd say to herself. And I would pretend that I hadn't heard her.

I also loved to eat *kodukkapuli* fruit; I liked the way it tasted.[1] There were many tall *kodukkapuli* trees, full of fruit, growing within our school compound. Even before the fruit had ripened, small chipmunks and bats would gnaw on that fruit and let it fall to the ground. The chipmunks would never eat what had already fallen to the ground. All of it would just lie there.

One day, both my elder brothers came up to Amma. "Amma, wake us up early tomorrow morning, will you? We're going to gather some *kodukkapuli* fruit," they said.

"*Dey,* don't ask me to wake you up so early in the morning!" Amma said. "See, even now, there are ghouls listening to what you're saying. Early in the morning, they'll come to you, looking just like me. They'll wake you up and take you off somewhere," she warned them.

There were so many beliefs back then about ghouls, goblins, and ghosts. But even at that age, I wasn't afraid of such things. When they went the next morning to look for *kodukkapuli* fruit, I went along with them. Why worry about ghosts and all such things?

I was in the third grade when Amma died. I must have been eight years old. She was still very young when she had her eight children, year after year, one by one. Her health must have suffered. She must have become quite weak with all those children to look after and no one around to look after her. Amma was always very ill.

Then there were all the troubles that came with the superstitions of that time.

When someone gets sick, they ought to be treated by a doctor. In the villages around Pudur back then, there were country doctors who would prescribe herbal medicines of various kinds. Prepare these medicines properly, and they could also work.

But when Amma got sick, no one did this for her. They took her to a soothsayer instead. He beat on his drum and examined her fortune. Then he told her that she had to bathe in water from head to toe. "Pour nine buckets of water over yourself, and you'll feel fine," he said.

Amma did just as he said. On the first night that she was sick, she poured water over herself. She was in a lot of pain and couldn't keep her food down. She couldn't walk, couldn't speak. By the next afternoon, she was dead.

This is all I know about her death. Why she was sick, why she died, I have no idea. I was studying in school at that time. Appa happened to be home then, in Pudur—it was one of those times when he'd come back from Burma. He had bought some land, a field with black soil fit for growing cotton. There were laborers that he'd hired to harvest cotton from that field, and he had gone out there to parcel out some cotton to give to each of them as a wage.

This was when, back at home, Amma had just died. They came to school to fetch me. "We just need to see your father. Show us where he is, will you?" they asked me. I left school with them and took them to that cotton field. There, they told Appa what had happened. Only then did I know why they'd asked to see him.

I didn't know or understand anything back then. You may not believe this, but I wasn't even sad when Amma died. I didn't feel anything, although she had just left us all behind. In those days, when someone in your family died, all your relatives would give you new clothes to wear. Actually, it was happiness that I felt when I received those new clothes. For the first time, I had something good to wear.

"Something terrible has happened, I ought to feel sad"—this is what I should have told myself. But these were things I never understood back then.

With Amma gone, feeding us and looking after the house became a problem. Appa kept going back to Burma. He arranged a marriage for my eldest brother, so that there would be someone to look after the family. But my sister-in-law didn't take care of us all that well.

For some time, my grandmother lived with us. The youngest of the children, my brother Raja, hadn't yet been weaned. What to do for milk? We had no milch animals at home at the time, no cows or anything like that, but my grandmother had a buffalo. She led that buffalo by foot all the way from Vaduvarpatti to Pudur and kept it there with us.

For a while, she raised us all, milking that buffalo each morning for something to feed my brother with. Then she also went back to her village, and Veda Nadar, my father's younger brother, stayed with us to help for some time.

My younger sisters suffered the most. Did someone ever say to them, "Look, the school is right here; go study for a while and come back home"? There was no one around to dress them in a skirt and blouse and send them off to school. They would tear off cloth from one of Amma's old saris to wrap around their waists. This was how they grew up. No school, at all.

In 1927, Appa built a house of his own, which was where we went to live when I was in the fourth grade. It was a tiled house, with stone walls for the first three feet from the ground, then baked mud walls rising up to the roof. Everyone said that Appa should marry once more, but he refused to take on another wife. "With seven or eight children already, how can I possibly marry again?" he would ask. "Suppose I have more children. How could I raise them?"

No one thought of family planning back then.

I was never a peaceful child. Often, I'd get very angry. I was once so furious that I grabbed a sickle and went after one of my older brothers. What had he done to make me so angry that I chased after him with a sickle? I can't remember. But I do remember how afraid he was when I chased him like that and how quickly he ran away. Anyway, it was just a small sickle, just what I happened to grab at that moment, that was all.

Those days, we weren't afraid of anyone else. Everyone else was afraid of us. In the village, our family was known as the *Veda kootam,* the "Vedar clan."[2] This meant that we were rowdies. The whole place would shiver at the sight of my uncle Veda Nadar, my father's younger brother. When he left the house, all the people of that village would shut their own doors, that's how much he terrified everyone. They were all a little scared of the Vedar clan.

Whenever Appa was in Burma, my uncle looked after the house. He was the one responsible for us. *"Dey!* Don't ever come home with a beating from any other kid at school!" he'd tell us. He didn't want us to come complaining that some other boy had hit us. "You hit him and then come home! Don't ever come here crying that you've been beaten by him," he'd say. This was how he raised us. This was how we learned to live.

When it came to causing trouble, my uncle was a master. He terrorized everyone, carrying a big staff wherever he went, setting fire to their stacks of hay. "Hey, where were you just now? What were you just doing?" he'd ask. Give him the wrong answer, and he would beat you. I don't know why he was like this, but this was how he lived.

The Nadar community organization called on him to try to stop him from behaving like such a rowdy. They wanted him to ask for forgiveness from the whole village, during a village council meeting, before the Bhadrakali Amman temple. But my uncle refused to come, and Appa had to appear before them, to ask for forgiveness on his behalf.

"You have to pay a fine of 1,000 rupees for these offenses," the leaders of the village council told Appa. But where could he go, in those days, for 1,000 rupees?

"We can't pay that much, we don't have that kind of money," Appa said.

"Then you have to pay 500 rupees," they said.

"Where can I go for 500 rupees?" Appa asked.

"Fine, pay 100 rupees. And if you can't do that, just get lost somewhere," they said. And when Appa refused once again to pay, they cast the whole family aside.

When the Nadar association did this, no one in the village was allowed to talk to us. Everyone else, aside from these two brothers and their families, had come together against us. The school, the common well, all of these belonged to the village as a whole. Now, with this decision, we could no longer enter that school or draw water from the common well. Though we were Nadars ourselves, we couldn't study in the Nadar school. We couldn't even approach the village Bhadrakali Amman temple. This was what they decreed.

Because they cast my father aside, my schooling also came to an end. I was still a young boy, maybe thirteen years old, studying in the eighth grade, when I was forced to leave school. I didn't understand what was happening. The school correspondent came to me and said that I couldn't come to school any longer. When even he had consented to this decision, what could I do? These were the rules of the village, and we had no choice but to accept them.

The school's headmaster, G. Victor, also lived in Pudur. He was a Christian. Whenever he walked past our house, he would always look very closely inside, to try to see how I was doing. Sometimes, he'd call out to me. "Come with me, boy," he'd say and take me along with him as he walked. I think he may have done this because he felt sorry for me, because the whole village had come together to cast us aside. "He's a good boy; it's too bad he can't study anymore," he might have thought to himself.

The headmaster could have tried to convince them to let me study, but they wouldn't have listened to him anyway. Teachers had to follow the dictates of the village. They had to respect what had been decided. When they kicked me out of school, I had to stop studying.

Whether I was upset or not that I couldn't go to school, I can't remember. At that age, you don't know what you've lost. It wasn't just that I didn't think much about this, about not being able to study anymore. I wasn't even concerned about my two younger sisters, who had no one to buy them something to wear and to send them off to school in the first place.

At the time, we were very poor. I had no dreams for the future, no hopes of becoming this, becoming that. Those weren't the kind of thoughts that children like me could have back then. "I should live like that . . . I should be like this . . . I should become someone like this . . ."

For about ten days, I just did nothing in Pudur. Then, Appa suddenly got a letter from my two older brothers in Burma. Appa had taken them to Burma to work in the shop at a very young age. I had another uncle there, Appa's younger brother Muthiah Nadar. My brothers used to work for him, but after a while, they wanted to stop. They wrote to Appa: "Uncle is too hard on us. We don't like being here anymore. Can you please do something about him?" Appa knew he had to go back right away. And when he went to Burma, he took me along as well.

When we left, Veda Nadar stayed on in Pudur, paying no attention to the decisions made by the village council. Everyone in the village got together to talk, and they decided to teach him a lesson. "How long will we have to be afraid of this one fellow? Who can live with someone like this? Let's take care of him." They waited for the right moment, and those with money paid off the police, so they wouldn't respond to what they had planned.

There was a common well in an orchard nearby. Veda Nadar had climbed down into that well to bathe, when ten or twenty people came in a crowd to take care of him. They surrounded him, standing all around that well with staffs, sickles, and axes. When my uncle began to climb out of the well, they pelted him with rocks that tore into his head and arms. Somehow, he managed to clamber out of the well. But as soon as he got out, they all struck at him together, breaking his arms and legs, leaving him lying there on the ground.

Appa got the news by telegram in Burma. He was very upset to learn what had happened to his younger brother. Leaving me behind in Burma, he took the first ship back to India. By the time he reached Pudur, they had already carried my uncle to a hospital in Ettayapuram.

At the hospital, they looked after him well. His wounds healed, and he was able to come back home again. From then on, my uncle always walked with a limp. But the problem in the village had been put to rest.

༄

# PUDUR, 2012

5

The imposing facade of the Hindu Nadar Primary School looms over the small dirt lane. The two entrances to the school open out onto either side of what was once the village's main bazaar, now quiet, nearly still. Built into the thick whitewashed walls are small alcoves for candles—empty now, they look like ornamental motifs.

The bazaar was once bustling with trade in grain, cloth, and other goods, and there is wealth still evident in the way that the main school building was built in 1920: the peacocks carved into wooden supports for the rafters, the thick pillars flanking one entrance, the elaborate flowers carved into the blue lintels above the many smaller doors.

In this village, like so many others nearby, the school was financed and built by a Nadar community association. These associations relied on the wealth newly accumulated by traders and merchants of the community: in village bazaars like that of Pudur, in the new market towns that began to develop in the late nineteenth century, in the mercantile networks that sent men like Ayya's father to overseas colonies such as Burma and Malaysia. These associations insisted upon strict codes of collective discipline. This was how they had stewarded the transformation of a disdained community of toddy-tappers into an upwardly mobile population.

Within the school compound, boys and girls in brown uniforms gather under the shade of a few neem trees. They bend close over their textbooks and notebooks, some in English, most in Tamil. It was here, within the sheltered space of the same schoolyard, that Ayya began each day with that song of praise—

> God save our gracious king
> Long live our noble king
> God save our king . . .

Standing there now, I can almost hear the youth in his voice once more: the even cadence of his singing, the rising pitch of certain notes, the breathlessness of one long line, as though all the dashed hopes of that time remain buried in these English words.

But there's little time to contemplate such things. The school manager is suspicious of my presence. Ayya might be the oldest surviving student of the school, as I suggest to him, but the manager doesn't seem that impressed.

He points out all the new buildings that have been raised in recent years, hemming in the original expanse of the school's grounds. The almond and *kodukkapuli* trees are gone. Nothing of that time remains, he insists.

This isn't the first time I've visited Pudur. I remember the children in ragged clothes, distant cousins, cheering and crowding around our van some thirty years ago. Then there was that visit about a decade ago, the day after one of my childhood friends had killed himself in Los Angeles. I can still picture the posters on his bedroom walls: the Porsche Carrera, the Ferrari Testarossa, the Wall Street skyline. Totems of our American childhood in the 1980s, these same things propel the ambitions of so many young men in India now.

The village of Pudur lies ten kilometers from a national highway. It was always a bumpy ride, but the blacktop now is new and smooth, broken only by the bundles of grain laid out on the road for passing cars to thresh. Trucks carrying massive rings and spokes rocket along the highway, bound for the windmills rising from the arid brushlands to the distant south.

It's a dull green landscape between the city of Madurai and the village of Pudur, mostly occupied by another twentieth-century immigrant from America: *Prosopis juliflora,* the hardy and voracious mesquite tree. As the car speeds along the road, the shrubs bleed into a uniform blur. On the highway these days, it takes little more than an hour to make the journey from country to city. And aspirations for development lead there, and much farther away.

ᰔᰕ

# A DECADE IN BURMA

# 6

BURMA WAS WHERE MY FATHER LEFT ME. I COULDN'T IMAGINE
what this "Burma" was or how it looked. I didn't even know that it
was a different country. There was a place called Burma, and Appa's
shop was there—that was all I knew. I never asked Appa anything
about Burma, when he came back to Pudur, and there was nothing
that Appa would ever say. As far as I can remember, not once did he
bring back something for us to play with from there.

Burma . . . Until then, I hadn't even been to Madras or Madurai.
People from Pudur sometimes went as pilgrims to the Murugan
temple on the seashore, in Tiruchendur, but I hadn't even been there.
I never went far from Pudur. And wherever I went, it was on foot, or
by bullock cart: no bus, no train, nothing like that. To Burma, you
had to go by ship, but until then, I'd never even seen the sea.

From Pudur, we went to a place called Pandalkudi, a slightly
bigger village some seven miles away. For a quarter of a rupee, a
bullock cart carried us there with all our things and left us at a stand

for horse carriages. From there, it was another eight miles to Arup-pukottai. We had to wait there in the sun, beside those carriages, until enough people had drifted by, also wanting to make that trip. Sometimes, this could take all day, and we waited until the afternoon or evening for a horse carriage to Aruppukottai.

None of this I had seen before. From Aruppukottai to Madurai, we went by bus, and then we took the train from Madurai to Madras. What I remember about that first train journey is that it was very crowded. So many others jammed into those seats, so many bedbugs hiding in the cracks and crevices of those wooden benches. We were bitten all the way to Madras.

When we got to Madras, we went straight to the port. There were agents there to help travelers going to Burma. You could approach one of them, and he'd buy you a ticket and take you to the right ship. At the time, a ticket from Madras to Rangoon cost just sixteen and a quarter rupees. Because Burma and India were both ruled by the same government, we didn't need a passport, or visa, or any such documents to go there.

It was just as we travel now from Madurai to Madras, that three-day journey by ship from the Madras port—that's how routine the trip was back then. For me, however, all of this was a strange and marvelous experience. The ship was just a small steamer. I could see the water twenty feet below the deck. As we went, I kept looking down at the sea. There were crabs and fish in the waves. There were even fish that leapt up above the water.

We had some sambar rice and tamarind rice with us, wrapped up in bundles of cloth. With just a little salt and chili pepper, that tamarind rice would last without spoiling for two or three days. People with money traveled by second class, with their own rooms and a comfortable bed to sleep on. We went by ordinary class.

It was dirty where we slept. As the ship tossed up and down on the waves, people were vomiting all around us, wherever they were sleeping. But nothing like this happened to me. I was used to wandering around under the sun, among the thorns and shrubs, with nothing at all to wear on my feet. I was used to drinking all kinds of water: when it rained in Pudur, I would just drink out of gullies on the side of the road, using my hands to push aside the dirt. This must have been why I never got sick on that ship.

We left the ship at the town of Rangoon. What was it like to see that town for the very first time? For someone who had never seen such things, Rangoon looked like a heavenly place. Who could imagine such a city? Everything was new and beautiful: the trams, the motorized coaches, the railways, all of this was a wonder.

Everyone there looked different too, all of them looking after their own work. In Rangoon back then, there were more Indians than anyone else. We knew a Muslim man who used to supply Appa's shop with provisions. He was originally from the village of Ilaiyangudi, close to Pudur. We went straight to his shop from the port, and he fed us well. We stayed with him in Rangoon for just one day, and then we left for Okpo, by train.

Okpo was a small town. There weren't that many houses there, and they were all built with wood, cut from a forest about twenty miles away. Teak wood was plentiful in Burma—as everyone knows, the country was famous for its teak.

Okpo was surrounded by rice paddies, and its soil was rich and fertile. The town was close to the Irawaddy River, always flowing with fresh water. Those fields never needed fertilizers—to harvest the rice, they would cut away the top half of the stalks and thresh these for rice. Then they'd set alight and burn what was left on the ground. The ash made for a good fertilizer. They would plow it into the soil, water the fields, and then raise another crop. Rice grew well in Burma, and it sold cheaply, too.

The town had a railway station, and there were many government officers who lived there: Burmese people, but also Tamils and Telugus from India. Others who lived in Okpo came from Orissa, Kerala, Gujarat, and many other places. Seven or eight Nattukottai Chettiar families[1] had settled there, each in huge bungalows of their own. There weren't many other Nadars in the town, just one or two others aside from us. And you couldn't find a single British person living there. They needed more comfort than the town could provide.

We stayed together in one large house. There were no individual rooms, just a long hall, both upstairs and downstairs, where we could stack up as many goods as we needed to store. Two truckloads of goods would fit within that house, there was that much room inside. Appa's shop was right there as well, kept on the veranda in the front. There was an awning stretched over it; we would close off one side to store the goods and do business on the other side. The kitchen was in the back, and that was also where we slept.

One of my uncles was with us there, Muthiah Nadar, Appa's younger brother. He was a talented trader and managed to make a fair amount of money. He bought a horse, which he would ride around to collect what others owed him. One day, he tied up that horse outside a large store owned by one of the Chettiars in Okpo and went off somewhere else. I saw the horse and cut it loose, climbing on top. Just like that, it began to trot away. I didn't know what to do. Finally, the horse stopped by itself at another stand, and I climbed down. The shopkeepers stared at me—"Look at this small boy riding that horse!" they said, shocked by what they saw.

Muthiah Nadar was married to a woman named Dhanabakkiyam. This aunt was very fond of me, as loving as a mother ought to be. She wasn't Burmese herself but a Tamil woman born in Burma. She even gave me a Burmese name, Maung Chit Pyon. All young children are called "Maung" in Burmese. Adults are called "Ko," and elders are called "U." This name, Maung Chit Pyon, was meant for someone who always smiled, it seems. In the time that I spent there with my aunt, I managed to learn a little Burmese.

Like a son of her own—that was how she treated me. When I first came to Okpo, I always stayed beside her, always ate with her. Once, I remember, she had asked me to slaughter a chicken. I stepped onto that chicken with my legs, held it firmly, and cut its neck with a long, curved knife. Suddenly, there was blood every-where. I tossed the head away and watched as that chicken's body kept quivering. I felt terrible. "Here's this life, quivering, this thing

that I've killed," I thought to myself. Not once did I slaughter a
chicken after that.

The Burmese would never eat what they'd killed themselves. They
ate chicken, duck, and fish but never killed these animals on their
own—they'd always buy and eat only what others had killed and
brought to sell. From then on, I also did the same.

It was in Burma that I first learned how to do business. Until
Appa came back again from India, Muthiah Nadar managed the
shop. He was a difficult man to work for. Everyone had to do exactly
as he said. "Do this, boy!" he'd say, and this is just what you did, or
else he'd force you to do it. I always obeyed his orders, but my elder
brothers didn't like this at all. They were the ones who asked Appa
to come back to Burma from Pudur. When my father returned to
Okpo, he split off his own business from his brother's. "You trade on
your own, and I'll do business with my sons," he told him. Muthiah
Nadar opened a shop of his own, as Appa had asked him to do, and
we looked after our shop together.

Muthiah Nadar didn't teach me very much about the business.
There was another man working in the shop for Appa, Chelliah Nadar, who taught me how they ran that shop. He was a distant relation,
an uncle to me. He worked in the shop for a salary and always ate at
our house. I assisted him for awhile, and he would tell me everything:
what something was called in Burmese, how much it sold for, how to
deal and trade in goods, what to do to earn a profit, and other details
of their daily transactions. Slowly, I learned how to trade on my own.

Chelliah Nadar was also the one who really taught me how to
speak Burmese. We knew many other traders, and we'd have to
speak with them in the Burmese language—otherwise, we couldn't
deal in goods. Day after day, as I listened to Chelliah Nadar speak,
I learned more and more Burmese. I learned how to pick out letters
in Burmese books and newspapers. And as soon as I was able to read
some of these words, I began to understand how to write Burmese.
Putting together one word after another, I learned how to read and
write in this new language.

We had a provisions store that sold all kinds of goods: stationery, household items, tubs and buckets, and other such things. We traded in rice and other things to eat like fruit, dried and salted fish, and vegetables. All of this we would measure out by the *visai*, in the Burmese way: there, one *visai* amounted to 1,400 grams. People would ask for a quarter of a *visai*, half of a *visai*, three-quarters of a *visai*, of something or another, which is what I learned to give them. This was how I got accustomed to the trade at Appa's shop.

The things we sold came from many different countries. Rice, lentils, beans, and teak grew in Burma—everything else was imported from abroad. You could buy a hundred *visai* of Javanese sugar for fifty rupees. Many other things came from India and China, such as the Chinese paper and stationery that was cheaply available. We couldn't import any of this into Burma ourselves. There were many Chinese also living in Burma, and those living in Rangoon would arrange to import these items. We would go to Rangoon to purchase goods and bring them back to sell in Okpo. Sometimes, they would send these goods to us from there.

In those days, the British had captured and ruled over many countries around the world. They refused to teach manufacturing techniques to anyone else. Not a single person in these various places knew how to make something as small as a needle, even. Even these tiny things, needles and pins, had to be imported from somewhere else back then. We didn't have the faith in ourselves to trust that we could make such things on our own. During those days of British power, people knew how to cultivate the land, but no more. Only later, after we had won our independence from them, did we learn some of these other trades ourselves.

Many things would come to Burma by ship. They would send over old newspapers from New York, to sell here for money. That paper was very cheap to buy and good for folding and wrapping other goods for sale, so we would buy some of it to bundle up things from the shop. The newspapers were printed in English; they made very little sense to me, as I hadn't studied very much English at the time, but I remember looking at those pictures.

Whatever goods we sold always went for a very low price. There was never much business at the shop: each day, we would sell only some forty or fifty rupees in goods. Once in a while an inspector, an Englishman, would visit the shop and examine what he had. We'd try to speak with him as best we could, about what we were selling, how many of us worked there, and so on. He would take a look at our account books and then go somewhere else.

Burma was where my father died. I was around fifteen years old at the time. When Amma died, I had felt no sadness—I was still a very small child. But Appa's death was hard on me. I didn't eat; I grew very thin. Appa was the one who sustained us all; we had no one else for support. There were seven of us children: I had two elder brothers, two younger sisters, and two younger brothers. Three of us brothers were in Burma, and the rest of the children were in Pudur.

Appa had been sick for a while, and we tried to look after him as best we could. Then he began to vomit up blood, again and again. There was a Muslim doctor nearby, and we took him to that doctor for treatment. Still, he wouldn't stop vomiting blood.

"I won't survive; I'm going to die," he finally realized. He asked the three of us to come to him. "I'll be gone, but I want the three of you to grow up well and to make a good living," he said. "Look after the shop. You'll have to be responsible for it. Don't forget your younger sisters and brothers—you'll have to look after them, too."

Mutharasu and Gurusamy were my brothers in Burma. I don't remember him saying anything about Mutharasu, but I remember him saying this about Gurusamy: "When he asks for his share of the property, he'll ask for a little more than he should—just give it to him."

About me, he said this: "He's a good one, a responsible lad. Look after him well."

Then there was my uncle Veda Nadar. He had beaten up Appa twice before, but Appa still loved him dearly. "Look after him too," he told us. Even though the man had beaten his own elder brother, twice, Appa's heart still melted at the thought of him.

When he died, I was at our second shop, in the Okpo bazaar. When they came and told me what happened, I tossed some sacks over everything in the shop and rushed back home. As soon as I got there, I started to cry. I was very upset for more than a month. I lost a lot of weight. There was a Tamil man, Hussein, who ran a fabric shop nearby. "Your little brother is always crying," he told my brother. "Try to keep an eye on him." That sadness stayed with me for some days longer, and then, little by little, it began to clear.

My eldest brother was twenty years old at the time; the next one was eighteen. They were the ones responsible now for everyone else in the family. They had studied only until the fifth grade, while I had studied up until the eighth. Both of them knew how to write, but still, when the time came to write Appa's name on his tomb, I was there to help. I remember the man who carved his name onto the tomb. He was a Hindi speaker. "You write it out in your language, and I'll make sure to copy it properly onto the tomb," he told me. And this was just what he did—the Tamil letters came out cleanly, well.

Now that Appa was gone, we had to take up the business and all its responsibilities. "We're used to doing this anyway. We'll manage to do a good job," we tried to tell ourselves, and we continued to trade in my father's name. In Burma, this is what they would always call Appa: M. P. Nadar. Mail that came to the shop was always addressed to M. P. Nadar, and those who sent us their goods would also use this name.

The wholesale dealers who supplied our shop continued to send us whatever we wanted. They sent us their goods on credit and took back what they were owed once we'd collected enough to repay them. It was these wholesale dealers who renamed our business "M. P. Nadar and Sons" after Appa died. They did this on their own, writing this trade name onto the invoices they sent us. They must have planned this together. "Their father has died, but his sons are there," they would have thought. They realized that we needed money and responsibility.

Children are responsible for the wealth of their fathers, but also for their debts. Should these goods be given out on credit or not?

How much could you give out on credit, and to whom? These were the kinds of questions that we learned to ask. We were honest in giving and taking, and we dealt well with whatever we were given. Slowly, we expanded the business, and we began to make a small profit on what we sold.

I liked living in Okpo. No one there would try to fool anyone else. There weren't many beggars in that town, and if someone was hungry, begging for food, there was always someone else who was willing to feed that person.

If you needed a bicycle in Okpo, you could rent one for a quarter rupee per hour. I would often ride into the countryside on a bicycle, just to look around. Many of our shop customers lived out there, and I would go off to visit them. They were very friendly with me—whether you were Burmese or Indian, guests there were always treated with a lot of respect.

Of course, if a Burmese person was angry, he would hit you or come after you with a sickle. They could also get quite angry, the Burmese.

We often went to Rangoon to buy supplies for the shop. During those days of British rule, Rangoon was a beautiful place. Everything there looked marvelous to my eyes: the houses, the shops, the cinema theatres. The trams were quite a sight too. We could climb onto them wherever we wanted, pulling ourselves up by rope. We would give a signal when we needed to get off the tram and hold onto that rope as we climbed down.

There were people from all over the world in that city: Japanese, Chinese, Indians, British . . . The British ran many big companies in Rangoon, like the company that sold us the fire insurance policy for our shop. There was a large wholesale general store, M. T. Sikkandar Baba and Co., owned by our Muslim friend from Ilaiyangudi. That was where we'd stayed when we first came to Rangoon from Pudur. They would sell us sack after sack of wholesale goods. We would also buy goods from Chinese traders, but whatever they sold was always for cash, never on credit. It was cheaper to buy from them, but so much of what they sold was poor in quality.

Competing with the Chinese were the Japanese shops. Even back then, they were known for making quality things. One Japanese agency in Rangoon sold Pilot pens. When people gathered around in a big crowd, these Japanese sellers would take out one of those pens and throw it against a wall. The tip of the pen would just stick into one of those wooden walls, without falling down, that's how strong those Pilot pens were. They convinced me to become an agent myself, and I took twelve pens from them. I sold all of them quickly, for three or three and a half rupees each. Some of those pens even had nibs made of gold, but they would sell for a higher price.

When it came to buying things or selling things, there was nothing like a standard price. We sold at the prices that everyone else was selling at—we set our prices based on what others were doing themselves. Otherwise, no one would buy from us. That was the time of the Great Depression, but I didn't know very much about what was happening around the world. Our business also dropped at that time; nothing would sell, and what sold would sell only very cheaply. Onions that used to sell for four annas per *visai* would sell for only three or three and a half annas.[2] That was all I understood about the depression.

Around that time, a shop in the Okpo bazaar came up for bidding. The auction was run by the town government; they were asking for less than nine rupees each month in rent. It was a big shop, so big that you could fill it with as many things as you wanted to sell. We took out a lease on that shop, in my name, and I began to tend to the business there. The shop was fine to look at, and you could see it very clearly from the main road in town.

The bazaar would open each morning at 6 AM and close each evening at 6 PM. The town appointed watchmen to look after the shops, and they were the ones who closed the gates each evening. No one could enter the bazaar after that time: even the merchants had to wait until the next morning to enter their own shops. We were allowed to do business for only those twelve hours each day.

I had many customers in that shop in the bazaar. Many of them were villagers who had come to Okpo to buy what they needed, just as they do here in India. At times, someone would ask for something that I didn't stock at the shop. I would run to the other shop we kept to try to get it for the customer. Business was good. I managed to save some money—actually, this was something that I learned to do quite well.

When it came to giving and taking, I learned what I had to do to make a profit. I had a sense for what had to be done, and when, in order to earn some money: how much to buy of one thing, how little to buy of another thing, how much more to order of something else so that some stock would remain in the store. I knew what to sell at what price, what would sell in what season, and what wouldn't sell at all at that time.

Neither of my elder brothers was very good at this. Both of them would take out loans to stock their shop with goods, without this sense of what would and wouldn't sell. They would ask a money-lender for a loan, and he would immediately give them what they wanted. But then, after a month or two had passed, they would have to pay him back. And meanwhile, those things that never sold would just lie there, month after month and year after year. "So what, let it lie there," my brothers would say, and let it go. They traded as they wished in Appa's old shop, while I ran that new shop in the bazaar properly. Things kept going somehow.

When it comes to keeping a shop, you generally need money to stock goods in advance. But because Appa had been trading there for so long, other merchants would lend him as much as he wanted on credit. We also didn't need to pay cash in advance for their goods. The wholesale merchants were willing to lend us as much as we would take. When it came to the business of giving and taking, we held to Appa's principles, and they trusted us because of his honesty.

My younger sisters and brothers were still back in Pudur. We would send them some of what we saved, for their expenses, always as money orders through the post office—they took a one-rupee commission for every hundred rupees we sent. The postal service in Burma was just like the Indian postal service. Offices, laws, all these were the same in both India and Burma.

One year I went back to Pudur, just for a short visit to see everyone. When I went, I remember, there was a ballpoint pen tucked into
my shirt pocket. At that time, no one had ever seen this kind of pen
before. It hadn't been introduced yet in that part of India, and there
was no way of buying one there. "Please give it to me, give it to me,"
so many people in the village said, but I refused to hand that pen
to anyone. "I can't do that," I kept telling them. I wouldn't even let
them try writing with it—if I did, I thought, they would keep it for
themselves.

Sometime after I returned to Burma once again, both of my
younger sisters came of age. Marriages had to be arranged. My eldest
brother, Mutharasu, came back to Pudur to try to find husbands for
each of them, but he didn't have a good sense of what to look for in a
groom. It seems that a soothsayer had told him that one of my sisters
had to be given to someone as a second wife. Just a superstition, that
was all, but my brother did exactly this, marrying her to someone
who had already been married once before. Later, we found out that
the man was someone who had fallen in love with a Burmese woman
and that he'd already had a child with her.

In Burma, you could take up with whomever you wanted, however
you wanted. It wasn't as though you had to get married. There were
no rules to follow. Burmese and Indians would often get together—
this was all very common back then. That was how that man had
taken up with a Burmese woman, and they wound up having a son
together. Then he took that child and came running back to India,
without even saying a word to that woman.

My brother Gurusamy's wedding took place in Burma. We never
had to search out a bride for him. There were many Indians who had
settled there with their families—like one of Appa's nephews, who
had been very close to my father. He came and told us that there
was a girl he knew who was suitable for marriage, someone whom
Gurusamy could marry. At the time, there was no one else around to
advise us about such things.

They lived in Zeegong. The girl's father was wealthy: he had a
good business, and one of his own nephews was a very rich merchant

in Nathalin. The nephew had a truck of his own, that's how prosperous they were. Mutharasu thought that we would be lucky to have a girl from such a family for Gurusamy, and so he fixed the marriage.

The wedding took place at their house. There was nothing like a stage for the wedding, no religious rites they followed. I don't even think we gave any jewels to the bride. There was a marital necklace to tie around her neck and saris to exchange, that was all. Her brother Muruga Nadar was the one who planned and organized everything. Some people we knew, maybe ten or so of them, came there for the wedding. They were given tea when they arrived and a meal that afternoon. The next morning, they all went back to their own towns.

Gurusamy was four years older than me. In time, there in Burma, I also came of age. Of course when that time comes, you begin to think about girls, have feelings for them. Girls weren't kept bridled by their families in Burma like they were in India. There, they had all the freedoms that boys had. Some of them would also trade alongside me, in the bazaar. They would buy goods from my shop, and some of them kept shops of their own.

Those Burmese girls would talk to me, and some of them were willing to get quite close. But I always kept my distance. Though it was common to take up with women in Burma, this wasn't something that I did myself. I didn't indulge myself in illicit pleasures or relations; whenever I had such thoughts, I would try to control them. Even if some girl came looking for me, I would attend to my own work. That was how I lived back then—I saw nothing but my trade.

I was that passionate about the business. But, because I always worked for so many hours each day, at times I would have to do something else to relax. "Come, let's play some cards," my friends would say. We would play cards, table tennis, even soccer or basketball.

In those days, all my friends were Burmese, and I always passed the time with them. Sometimes, we would drink country liquor together. Distilled spirits were also available, but there was a British customs tariff on imported liquor. I knew someone who sold liquor on the black market, and I would sometimes buy a bottle to hide away in the shop, to drink a little, sip by sip. On the black market, a bottle of spirits cost just half a rupee.

I often wandered around with my Burmese friends. Once, we went to watch a movie in another town, a Burmese film called *Mau Patti,* which meant "The Courage of a Young Man." We went there by train, buying tickets on the way there but not on the way back. When we got back to Okpo, the officer checking for tickets discovered that we didn't have any. He was someone used to taking bribes, and he knew me well. He asked me for money.

"I don't have any money," I said.

"Ok, I'll get it from you at the shop," he told me, and he let us go.

There were many Buddhist temples in Burma, and those days, there were always many old and broken things for sale around each temple. Once, we went from place to place to buy some of these things. My Burmese friends never had much money, so I took what money I had, met up with three friends, and paid for whatever was needed. We gathered up all the used goods we could find outside each temple and took them to Rangoon to sell. But whatever we made that day didn't add up to more than the four of us had spent. No profit on that outing.

There was one friend I trusted more than anyone else—Ko Chit Pon was his name. Everyone called him *makkambuwe,* which meant "mustache-man" in Burmese. When the Second World War began, it was in his hands that I put the shop, the keys, and all my things, before I left for India. "Here, friend, here's the shop. Look after it. Give it back to me when I come back, if we manage to find each other once more," I said to him.

And then we left.

෮

OKPO, 1940

# 7

India, Burma . . . Each seems so distant from the other now—one a tumultuous democracy, the other still a military morass. We live in an era that takes national borders as sacred boundaries, as if simply crossing over is an act replete with peril and potential. We also understand the cultures that these borders enclose as concoctions of a unique flavor or essence, as if these countries were packages stocked side by side on a grocery shelf. But travel wasn't always policed so strictly. Nor was the commingling of social and cultural worlds.

For centuries, India has had religious, commercial, and political footholds in the lands of Southeast Asia. Think of the tributes paid to the medieval Tamil Chola dynasty by Cambodian and Malaysian kings. Or of the many coastal trading posts established by Muslim merchants from Gujarat. Or of the Buddhist temples of Pagan in central Burma, their walls inscribed with Sanskrit, Pali, and Tamil prayers.

Following a century of piecemeal conquests by the British East India Company, India was taken under the British Crown in 1858. Burma, lying beyond the Andaman Sea, was gradually annexed to British India by the Anglo-Burmese Wars of the nineteenth century. Tens of thousands of Indians migrated there by steamship each year from various eastern ports, doing everything from pulling rickshaws, working in docks and rice mills, trading in rice and other commodities, staffing railways and customs offices, and financing the development of rice paddy cultivation throughout the Irawaddy River delta. Ayya's father was one of these migrants.

What was it like to have a place in that emerging world? Like many other colonial capitals, Rangoon was a cosmopolitan wonderland for those who found a way to profit from its commerce. By the 1920s, most of its population hailed from diverse regions of India. Here and in the surrounding towns, marriages and liaisons between Indian men and Burmese women grew commonplace. Complex relationships of trust and debt unfolded between the kin networks that had led migrants here and among the mercantile networks that developed.

I've seen a fuzzy black-and-white photograph of Muthiah Nadar's old shop in Okpo. I can imagine Ayya standing under a low-slung awning just like that one, chatting with his customers, friends, and admirers as he measures out goods from similar sacks and woven baskets. Beyond this image, though, there's only one other tangible record that remains within reach, if I want to try to reconstruct and imagine the daily life of that time.

Ayya still has a small account book from one of his last years in Burma. The notebook is slender and square, its cover long gone and its pages crumbling. It was in such books that Ayya and his brothers would keep a record of their daily business transactions. This particular notebook was kept by Ayya and his brother Gurusamy for their eldest brother, Mutharasu, who was in Pudur at the time, and for the income tax officers who would inspect their shops and accounts on a regular basis. The notebook dates back to 1940 and covers each day in the month of January that year.

Each of these pages begins by naming their concern, sometimes in English, generally in Tamil: Okpo M. P. Nadar & Sons, General Merchants, or Okpo M. P. Mutharasu Nadar and Brothers. The transactions, recorded neatly in individual columns for receipts and payments, give a vivid picture of the social and material intricacies of that world. Consider, for example, what happened on January 16:

The day begins with a balance of 35 rupees in hand. E. M. Gurusami Nadar, who has a grain shop in Okpo, is paid 20 rupees. Another 20 rupees go to Ingo Ling, who has sent the shop goods on credit from Prome in the north. Someone else gets a loan of 50 rupees.

A clerk named Appana gets 15 rupees for managing the workers who load and unload their goods. A Chinese man named Koppiya is also paid 10 rupees. Ayya and his brother buy a small tin of 12 dozen Puli brand matchboxes for 17 rupees from someone else, and other miscellaneous goods worth 375 rupees. A car is rented to deliver these things to their two shops. Identified as R.C. 6705, the car is rented for 10 rupees.

Ayya also goes south to Rangoon to buy stock for the shops. He pays 146 rupees in cash to Muhammad Kasin and Co. in Rangoon, and the store gives him goods on credit worth 207 rupees. The Chinese merchants Pian Pi and Co., also in Rangoon, won't give Indian traders anything on credit, and so Ayya pays them in cash for other goods worth 196 rupees.

Three dozen batteries are purchased for 5 rupees. Then there's a purchase for nearly 37 rupees from a company named with a long string of initials: Ci. Mu. Ne. Pa. Mu. and Co. The letters are intriguing. They seem to represent five generations of business in Rangoon.

Another company supplies miscellaneous items for 53 rupees: beedies to smoke, tobacco powder, fragrant leaves to smoke with the tobacco, small lightbulbs from Japan, candles, and fixtures for kerosene lanterns. Ayya hires laborers to carry all this for a little more than 6 rupees.

Ayya spends nearly 3 rupees on his own expenses, recording the amount, but not the purpose, in the name of his eldest brother. It costs close to 4 rupees to travel from Okpo to Rangoon and back. The notebook says that he's eaten on this day for less than 2 rupees.

By the end of the day, one shop sells goods worth 30 rupees, and 40 rupees of goods are sold in the other. At the close of the day's accounts, the notebook shows a balance in hand of just 5 rupees.

Ayya explains all this to me one afternoon in Madurai, as we pore over the columns together. Then he pauses, fixing me a look. This is just an official account book, he finally admits. These were records manufactured for inspecting eyes. No doubt, something more would have been earned that day, and done that day, as with every other day that month.

᷍

# WHEN THE WAR CAME

# 8

WE WERE PROSPEROUS. WE HAD GOOD REPUTATIONS. ALL KINDS of people would come to the shop and ask for things in their own languages, and we would respond in those languages too. We talked to everyone, learned all kinds of things. We didn't feel like strangers in that country. But then, over time, our relations with the Burmese people began to suffer.

Something happened in 1938. A Muslim man had written a pamphlet criticizing the Buddhist religion. Burmese people were furious. Wherever you looked, they were attacking Indians, beating them up. There were many riots.[1] I was never caught in any of these riots myself, but I saw such things happen, even in Okpo.

I was at home one day, watching from a distance, as Burmese villagers approached the edge of the town. They were planning to riot in the town, to attack the shops and rob things. They had almost reached Okpo when policemen lined up to protect the town. Those constables were also Burmese, and so was the sub-inspector in charge of them all.

There must have been about fifty rioters, coming with sickles, sticks, staffs, and other weapons. Facing them on the road were about ten or twenty policemen, armed with guns. They looked out at the crowd and gave them a warning: "Look at this line we've drawn here. You can't cross it. If you do, we'll shoot you."

I still remember how angrily that crowd was yelling as they came. "We'll cross the road and pillage the town!" they shouted. Then the sub-inspector gave his orders to shoot. The constables pulled out their weapons and fired on them. Three or four people died right there. Everyone else ran away.

The policemen washed down the road so that you couldn't see the bloodstains. Then they also left. There was no one around to attend to the dead.

This didn't happen in our town alone—it was like this everywhere. The Burmese began to speak very contemptuously about Indian people. "*Dey, kala!*" they'd call out, insultingly.[2] It was a harsh way of talking, a very disrespectful thing to say. Those who didn't have enough money to eat, those who did wage labor for a living, those who were willing to do anything to survive—at first, it was those kinds of people whom they would call *kala*. But then, over time, they started to say this about any foreigner, any Indian.

Some Burmese in Okpo even called me a *kala*, now and then. I don't remember exactly how this happened, but whenever I heard such a thing, I would turn around and head in some other direction. I couldn't face them and ask why they'd said this. We were in Burma, after all. There were always four or five of them, together, and if I said anything, they would beat me up. Sometimes, they would come to the shop, drunk, and ask for something. I had to give them what they wanted, or they would start a fight. All of this was hard on us. Our trade was going well, but when they began to call us *kalas*, we no longer got the respect that we deserved.

There was a man by the name of R. M. A. R. Lakshmana Chettiar in Okpo. There were many good things he'd done for that town. He installed a few hand pumps there, for example—I would always bathe beside one of those pumps. But much of Okpo's land was also in his hands. All the land around the town was in the hands of Indian Chettiars and the Chinese.

The Nattukottai Chettiars grabbed all that land by lending out money, again and again. They would lend to borrowers only if they mortgaged their land. Everyone there lived in wooden houses, and with so many trees around, there was no value in putting up their houses as security. Instead, they would have to put up their land, and if they couldn't pay back their loans, the lender would grab their fields.

The moneylenders brought their own laborers from India to cultivate the lands they had grabbed. This was what the Burmese hated the most. "They've taken our lands, they've taken our livelihood, soon they'll take our towns and villages away from us too," they thought.

The Burmese didn't blame the Chettiars alone. They thought that foreigners were doing this, that Indians were doing this. There was nothing there like caste. "It's the Indians who are lending out so much; they're the ones who are exploiting us," the Burmese felt. This was how that hatred of Indians began to develop. This was why all those riots took place.

Some of our own goods, we gave out on credit to our customers. Generally, they would pay us back, but if they didn't, we would have to let it go. "If he wants it for himself, let him have it," we would tell ourselves. We couldn't do anything to try to collect on those debts. After all, they weren't giving us gold as security for what they borrowed from us. We just wanted to sell our goods, that was all. All we could do was to raise our prices a bit for those who took things on credit—at least that way, we could make something of a profit.

In 1941, we finally closed down the shop in the bazaar. There wasn't much business there anymore, and what I earned didn't even cover the rent. There was another bigger town, Minhla, about fifteen miles away, where we knew a Nadar man like us, Kasi Nadar. He was a good man. He also had a provisions store, and he would come to us if he needed something to stock his own shop. Sometimes, he visited us at home. There was some fondness, some unity, among the Nadars there in Burma—after all, it was a foreign country. It was Kasi Nadar who came and told us that there was a shop vacant in Minhla.

I rented out that shop, filled it with things to sell, and began to trade there. A lot of what I needed was already in that empty shop, even a weighing scale. I didn't open up a new business account when I began to work there—I didn't even buy new account books. "Let's treat it as another branch," my brother Gurusamy said. He was never one to be satisfied with the business of just one shop; instead, he would try to get a foothold in many different places. He was the one looking after me back then, and so I did as he said, opening up another shop for us in Minhla.

At that time, I must have been about twenty-one or twenty-two years old. There was a Tamil restaurant in Minhla, with *idli, dosai,* and chutney to eat each morning.[3] For lunch and dinner, I would cook something at home. At the time, I hadn't yet begun to think that I ought to get married or go back to India. "Where else would I go? Why would I go to India?" I thought to myself.

In the end, though, I tended that shop in Minhla for just three months. When the war reached that town, I had to close up everything.

We knew the world war was coming. We knew everyone would have to pack up and go. I remember reading in the papers about the Japanese suicide bombers and about the *Victoria,* the British battleship that they attacked. At the time, it was the largest battleship in the world. The British had sent it to Singapore, and the Japanese had somehow gotten into its smokestacks and blown up the ship. It just sank, I remember.

Malaysia, Singapore, Kuala Lumpur, Penang . . . All these places, the Japanese took. One by one, they seized each place. Rangoon was the Burmese capital, and the Japanese struck very close by. Soon, they would take Rangoon, too.

Passage by ship was coming to a halt. My brother Gurusamy was worried. "We may not be able to go back to India," he thought. He didn't like the idea of being stuck in Burma. Somehow, he managed to get a ticket on the last ship leaving from Rangoon to India. He got onto that ship with his wife and went back home.

Mutharasu and I could have also gone with him on that ship. But we still had two shops here: all that business to look after, and whatever property we owned. We had no other way of making a living. How could we cast all this aside and just leave? "You go first; we'll come later," Mutharasu said to Gurusamy, and he and I stayed behind.

Then we got news that the Japanese were coming closer. We heard that Rangoon would fall in just two days. Even within Burma now, there were so many battles. No goods came from anywhere outside the country. Everything ground to a halt. We kept selling what we had stocked up in the shops. And then, just ten to fifteen days after Gurusamy had left, the Japanese captured Rangoon and all the surrounding areas.

Mutharasu was anxious. His wife and son were in Pudur, and she was due to have another child. The two of us were alone in Burma, with everyone else in the family back in Pudur. As the battles continued, Mutharasu grew more distressed. "Let's go," he finally told me, and took me along with him back to India. "We don't need these troubles for ourselves."

If my eldest brother hadn't been around, I would have stayed on in Burma by myself. He had a family of his own back home in Pudur. But where I was living made no difference to me. Many single people like me stayed on in Burma.

My brother, however, wasn't prepared to hear any such things from me. "The shop will remain here," he said. "If we come back, we can look after it once more." He was my eldest brother. I listened to what he said. And so we left everything behind and came away as refugees from Burma.

The trains were still running to the north. We took one of those trains, leaving all our things behind in Okpo. With us we had two trunks, packed with some clothes and other things. Everything else at the house, and in the shop, we left behind. We couldn't sell any of it—who would buy such things in wartime? These were losses on our accounts, that was all.

We gave over the shop and everything inside to that Burmese friend of mine, Ko Chit Pon. "Look after the shop, friend. If we ever come back, and if you've made any profit from the shop, just give us some of what you earned," I told him. Aside from him, we didn't tell anyone else that we were leaving.

Our train took us as far as Prome. There was a river flowing near the town, and across that river was a camp for the refugees traveling from here to India. They'd raised a large tent at the camp, and we stayed there for four days and nights, eating and sleeping under that tent. There must have been about 500 people also staying there at the time.

"How do you get to India?" we asked.

"You have to walk along a military road, through a jungle in the mountains," they told us.

The road stretched for a hundred miles, and going all that way on foot would have been very difficult. Those who were poor were just walking, but those with a little money had gotten bullock carts and loaded them with food and water to take along with them. There were no towns or stores or anything else along the way.

We thought we might be able to rent a bullock cart, but they were asking as much in rent as it would cost to buy a new cart and a pair of bulls. So we bought two bulls and a cart, loaded up our belongings, some things to eat, and water to drink, and drove that cart out of the camp. Sometimes we would climb onto the cart ourselves, and sometimes we would walk along behind it. That was a mountain path that we had to climb, just wide enough for a bullock cart to pass.

For seven days, we traveled like this. It was a terrible area to cross. Hardly anyone came or went along this route. There were no houses along the way. You couldn't get water, basic necessities, or anything at all to eat. There was only jungle, climbing high up and falling deep down once again, through endless thickets of bamboo. The military road was cut deep into that jungle, with mountains rising up on all sides. You could see streams flowing fifty feet down the slope. Poisonous plants of all kinds would drain into those streams, and the water was full of worms and bugs.

People can go without eating if they must, but no one can survive without water. Some of the other refugees had brought just a little water with them. When this ran out, they had no clean water with which to relieve their thirst. These people would scoop up water from a stream to drink. Then they would get diarrhea and struggle for their lives. This was what happened to a quarter or even half of those who came walking along that way.

Many of them, close to death, crowded both sides of the path with containers in their hands. *"Ayya,* water . . . *Ayya,* water . . ." they would beg those of us who were passing along that way on carts. No one would do anything to help them.

"Help them by giving up our own water, and we will suffer the same fate," those with water thought to themselves. They would keep on going, paying no attention to the others who were begging like this.

Wherever there was water running, wherever we lay down to sleep, we would find ten or even thirty bodies also lying there. We had to cook and eat right beside them. There were bodies lying right along the path, and the bullock carts were driven right over them. I remember how the feet of the bulls and the wheels of the carts would grind into those bodies as we passed. These were terrible things to see. This is what we had to cross to come back to India.

The government did nothing for us there. They didn't tell us to go this way, nor did they stop us from going this way. We were under British rule, and they were fighting with Japan at the time. Usually, back then, those with cholera or other such illnesses were not allowed to board ships or to travel along important routes. But here, along this path, no one asked us for medical certificates. We just kept going, on our own.

There were seven or eight men traveling with us who had been working with us for wages in Okpo. All of them were walking with us as we came along, but then, one among them got diarrhea and lost all his vigor. We didn't know what would happen to him. We were also afraid that if we carried him along with us, none of us might make it to India ourselves. And so we left him there, sitting up against a tree.

I have no idea what happened to him after we went on. He didn't come home alive. All his relatives were from a village near Kovilpatti. Once we reached Pudur, they came to ask about him, but we couldn't tell them the truth. "We don't know what happened," we said and left it at that.

"Just tell us whether he's alive or dead," they begged us. "If he's dead, we have to arrange for his last rites." But what could we say? "We just don't know," we replied.

What can I say about what I felt then, in my heart? Imagine how it must have been, to leave that life to struggle for survival without doing anything to save him. I was distressed by this for a long time to come. I can't recall that man's name, but his memory will not leave me.

Near the border between India and Burma was the town of Akyab. Now that we'd crossed the mountains and reached the seashore, we had to take a boat to get to Akyab. We waited a long time for a boat to come. When nothing came, we decided to sleep right there. There were two others with us who were also from Pudur, men who worked at the shop, I think. When my brother and I were asleep, they carried off one of our trunks and everything inside.

"Fine, what's gone is gone," Mutharasu and I told ourselves, and let it go. Luckily, all our money was tucked into our waists, still safely with us. We'd lost one of the two trunks that we had brought, but with the remaining trunk in hand, we caught a boat and headed for Akyab.

Bombs were dropping on that town when we landed there. All the big shops had been crushed and flattened. We saw one medical shop that had been bombed, with medicines lying scattered all around the ground outside. We could have taken as much as we wanted, that's how many medicines were lying there. But we didn't take any of it, just a large piece of canvas cloth that had fallen onto the ground, something we could spread out to lie down upon.

There was an arrangement to travel from Akyab by ship to Chittagong. People had already filled up that ship, and when we asked, they said that there was no more room on board. Somehow, I managed to find a place for Mutharasu and me. There were just two tickets left, and we would have to sleep on the floor, they told me.

"Just give them to us," I said and took those two tickets for me and my brother. "Find another ship for yourselves and join us back home," we told the others still with us, giving them some money for any expenses they might have.

We got onto that ship and made it to Chittagong. The Congress Party was strong there, and they had organized a powerful movement for Indian independence, against British rule. When we arrived in Chittagong, party workers came on their own to greet us. They escorted us off the ship, gave us a warm welcome, and led us to where we needed to go next.

Another ship took us from Chittagong to Calcutta. They accepted all of us on board as refugees without asking for any payment, without even asking our names. Once again in Calcutta, Congress workers welcomed us as refugees from Burma. "Victory for Mahatma Gandhi!" they called out at the railway station, as they gifted us with shawls. We had to take a train from there to Madras, and they gave us some rice, porridge, and biscuits to eat and water to drink on the train. They even bought our tickets for us.

In Madras too, party workers and government officers were there to help. They gave us a comfortable place to stay the night, fed us once more, and made arrangements for each of us to travel to our native places. They bought us each railway tickets and sent us off one by one.

When Mutharasu and I finally reached Pudur together, no one else remained with us. We had some clothes left in one trunk and some money tucked into our waists—that was all that we managed to bring back from Burma.

Happiness that we'd escaped with our lives, or sorrow that we'd lost everything we had—I felt none of this, then. I knew nothing about such happiness or such sorrow. I was glad to see my brothers, my sisters, and the children, but that was all. In those days, nothing else made much of a difference to me. I would eat whatever I got. I didn't crave rich food to eat, rich clothes to wear. "Look at how those guys are dressed; I don't have anything like that . . ." Such thoughts never crossed my mind back then.

We must have had about 2,000 rupees in hand when we left. We gave some of this money to those who came along with us, to meet their expenses along the way. Now that we had made it back to India, we gave some of what we still had to everyone else in the family.

I had no source of income, and I had to earn a living somehow. Because I liked to keep shop, my brothers set up a small provisions shop for me in Pudur. We had some ancestral land in the village, and we gave this to Mutharasu, to cultivate. We bought him new plow bulls and built a shed to keep the bulls. This was how we spent all the money we had in hand.

I didn't believe, back then, that I would ever go back to Burma. Until 1945, Burma was under Japanese rule. Residents had to use the Japanese currency; our money was worthless there. If I ever had gotten the chance to go back to Burma and take back the shop there, I might have taken it. But I didn't have that chance, and I didn't think twice about that loss.

When the war ended in 1945, the British took hold of that country once more. Many who had fled from Burma began to go back again. Mutharasu also went back and rented a shop to do business there once more. He took his whole family and stayed there for ten or fifteen years, finally returning to India when the Burmese military took over the government. They decided that Indian citizens would have to pay a special tax in order to do business in Burma. If Indian merchants had given out loans to farmers, they weren't allowed to try to collect them. These changes created a situation that made it impossible for my brother to stay there.

After the war, my younger brother Shanmugam also went for some time to Rangoon. His father-in-law had a shop there, and he went to help him out. Shanmugam went once to Okpo to pay his respects at our father's tomb. He even saw my friend Ko Chit Pon. There was a clock hanging on the wall of our shop there, and when Shanmugam came back to India, he brought the clock back with him. My other younger brother, Raja, saw it and took it for himself.

I didn't know that Shanmugam had brought that clock back to India. Two months later, I happened to see it, hanging on a wall in Raja's house. "Hey, this looks like the clock in our shop in Burma," I thought to myself. Only then did Raja tell me what had happened.

That was a Japanese clock, white in color. I'd bought it in Rangoon—it wouldn't have cost more than ten rupees. It wasn't even all that nice, that clock.

# KOVILPATTI, 1946

# 9

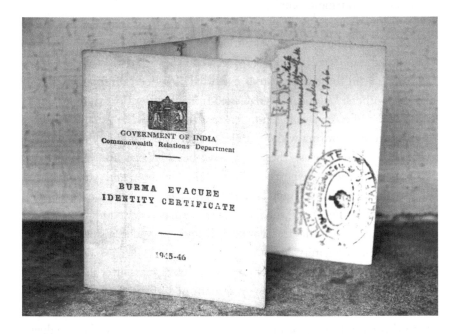

There is an invisible nation within the nation of modern India, one that will never rally under a common flag or celebrate the memory of a common heritage. I mean the multitudes of refugees scattered among the most crowded urban tenements and the loneliest corners of the countryside. Refugees from the cataclysmic tumult of the twentieth century. Refugees from floods, droughts, and other natural disasters of unnecessary gravity. Refugees from the forces of development that impoverish certain regions to fuel the prosperity of others.

These millions of men, women, and children may have much in common, when it comes to their experiences of displacement and neglect. But they are unlikely to see this in each other, due to the lines of social antagonism that led so many of them to flee from so many places. Take the Partition that split an independent subcontinent into two nations in 1947, engulfing millions of families in a spate of violence along the new boundaries between India and Pakistan. Or that other partition of British India in which my grandfather was caught, the geopolitical schemes that consolidated a Burmese state for Burmese people.

Collective violence is often imagined as something that happens in the absence of official oversight or attention: as a consequence of primitive and ungoverned impulses. There are, however, countless ways that modern states are complicit in these acts. Care is extended along certain lines, to the exclusion of others: Europeans were ferried from a falling Burma, for example, while others like Ayya were left to fend for themselves.

Ayya went to Burma without a passport and returned to India with no evidence of who he was. There may have been ledgers and registers that recorded his name at the ports in Chittagong, Calcutta, and Madras—after all, Britain had tried to impress upon India the ponderous importance of such documentation. But if such records were made, Ayya doesn't remember them. His account of that treacherous journey is pervaded instead by a sense of numberless anonymity.

In 1946, a year after the end of the war, and five years after these refugees flooded India from Burma, the government of India offered them "Burma Evacuee Identity Certificates." Those who knew of these certificates had to claim them at a local government office. Pudur belonged to the Kovilpatti Taluk of Tinnevelly District, and Ayya learned that others from the village were traveling to the taluk office to file an application. He also went along with them.

At the taluk office, Ayya was given a trifold strip of paper, stamped with the seal of the Kovilpatti taluk magistrate. He was identified on the certificate as Mariappa Nadar, MAD No. 23899: 28 years of age, male, and the son of Piraiyur Nadar. Two physical signs were cited on the document as identifying marks: the black mole on his right wrist, and the small scar that remained on his forehead from the day he had tripped and cut his head as a child at school.

The document was prepared by one P. C. Subbiah Mudaliar, a second-class magistrate. The officer accurately identified Ayya's three dependents at the time: his wife, a son, and a daughter. But for whatever reason, the magistrate took less care with another section of the certificate, meant to detail each refugee's "pre-evacuation interests in Burma." Here were the precise contents of the response handwritten onto those dotted lines:

(a) Stranded members of family + dependents
(b) Any other interests
(d) Prospects

What was happening at the taluk office that afternoon? It looks as though the officer at that desk simply copied down a list of prompts by rote, repeating them word for word on the form rather than using them as the basis to interview the former refugees and take down their answers—yet another absurd exercise of bureaucratic authority in the name of public assistance.

The certificate, in any case, was useless to Ayya. Certified refugees were entitled to a monthly stipend of thirteen rupees, if they were willing to travel each month to one government office to verify their identity and then wait at another office, the treasury, to collect the money. Two days were required to accomplish these tasks on each visit, as well as the expenditure of two or three of those rupees. Ayya never bothered to apply for anything more than the certificate itself.

There was also his father-in-law, who wouldn't have let him go like that to Kovilpatti each month. "We're running a cloth shop here, and my son-in-law wants to go get money as a refugee," the man might have muttered. And so Ayya always kept the certificate hidden from him. "Why did he get this, anyway?" Ayya worried his father-in-law would have asked him. "Maybe he'll take my daughter and run off with her?"

Displacement weaves the threat of betrayal into the texture of everyday life. For this reason, perhaps, Ayya kept this certificate of his refugee status locked away for many years, along with the story of how he'd earned it.

Then, one afternoon in Madurai, he took the yellow card out of an enameled tin box and handed it to me. "Look at this," he said, simply.

Sixty-six years had passed since the certificate was issued, but the paper was still crisp and smooth under my fingers. His story suddenly had a physical density I'd never felt, as though a map of his route through the Burmese mountains had unfolded between my hands.

༄

# A NEW LIFE AT HOME

# 10

I FELT BORED AND LISTLESS WITHIN A WEEK OF COMING BACK TO Pudur. I couldn't just sit at home. But there was nowhere to pass the time other than the village bazaar. I had an uncle named Gnani Nadar who had a shop in the bazaar. Each day I would go and sit on the steps at the entrance to his shop, just to watch what was happening. This uncle always spoke warmly to me, but he never offered anything to eat or drink—not even a bit of palmyra fruit, not even water.

Gnani Nadar made sesame oil to sell. There was a grinding mill at the Pudur *pettai*—pay the miller, and he would grind your sesame for you.[1] My uncle would buy some sesame, mix it with palm sugar, and grind it at the mill to measure out and sell. He often saw me in front of his shop and noticed how closely I'd been watching him do business. "Maybe he can help out," he must have thought to himself, because he asked me if I wanted to join him. I was doing nothing at the time, and so I went to work with him.

I would climb into his bullock cart to head to the weekly market nearby and come home once more in the same cart each evening. My uncle offered four annas for each day of work. It was very little, but I took it. That was how we did things in those days. I couldn't sit around doing nothing—I would work, even for just a single anna. "You've got to pay me this much" was something that I never said. He gave me what he wanted to give, and I worked as I wanted to work. That was all.

Each day at the market, Gnani Nadar would also give me one more anna to spend. "Go buy yourself something to eat," he'd say. I would wander around, looking at everything, but I would never spend that one anna. I would wait until I came home that night to have some rice and water—I always came back home with that one anna still in hand.

I went with him to the market like this for two or three weeks. I watched him dole out the sesame oil and collect money from his customers. "Get that for me, get this for me . . ." he would sometimes tell me. Whenever he stepped away for a little while, I would have to do exactly what he'd been doing. I carefully collected what people had paid and told him, when he came back, how much had been sold and for what price. And I gave him all that money.

Gnani Nadar watched me do all this. He saw how honestly I worked. Someone else might have sold something for eight rupees but given back only seven, keeping a rupee for himself, but I always gave him exactly what I'd been paid. In just those few weeks, Gnani Nadar began to appreciate my abilities as a trader.

At the same time, one of Appa's relatives approached us, offering her daughter in marriage. The girl's mother was related to us through Appa's grandmother. She had always spoken very respectfully to Appa—*annachi, annachi,* "elder brother, elder brother," she always called him. She was affectionate with all of us. There were two girls in that family, and Chellammal was the older of the two. In those days, girls were married off as soon as they came of age, or at least within a year or two of that. At that time, she was only fifteen years old. I was twenty-two.

By the time she was born, her mother and father, Chinnathambi Nadar and Pechammal, had been married for four years already. Everyone back then expected a child within a year of getting married. For this girl's parents, years had passed without a child. When she was finally born, they named her Muthu Karupayi, after her father's mother. Of course they couldn't say that name, out of respect to her grandmother, who was still alive. They may have also worried that if they called her Karupayi, she might turn *karuppu,* black. And so, because they had waited so long for her, and because they raised her with so much *chellam,* fondness, they began to call her Chellammal.

I knew her even before I'd gone away to Burma. She was much younger than me. She was always scared to see me and would run away and hide. She and her sister would have to walk past the front of our house to go to their family's orchard. They kept goats in their family, and those two girls, those sisters, would keep those goats close as they drove them toward the orchard. They would always pass along the lane in front of our house.

Whenever they did that, they would try to peek inside, to see what was happening within the house. Who knows, Chellammal may have even felt something for me back then. She was a dark girl, and I was fair-skinned. Back then, girls were easily attracted to boys they saw—it was nothing like what happens now. Older girls were never allowed to go to school, and they were always trapped at home. Chellammal's family allowed her to study only until the eighth grade.

Shanmugavel Nadar, Chellammal's uncle and her father's brother, was the eldest man in their family. He didn't have any children of his own. At first, he resisted the idea of marrying her to me. He had a cloth business in the bazaar, a small shop that he looked after with Chellammal's father, Chinnathambi Nadar. Shanmugavel Nadar probably thought something like this to himself: "This boy has just come back from Burma. What does he know? As soon as the war is over, he'll run off again to Burma, and what will our girl do then?"

There was another boy who was working in the shop—he must have been about two or three years younger than me. That boy had a lot of experience in the cloth trade, and he had been very loyal to Chellammal's uncle and her father. They planned at first to wed Chellammal to him, although he wasn't even related to them at all. They thought of this only because he was working for them.

Her mother was the hurdle to these plans. "He's my elder brother's son. We won't give our girl away to anyone else but him!" she declared. Our house was very close to theirs. She would often come by, insisting that I marry this girl. After some time, Gnani Nadar also came and spoke to Shanmugavel Nadar. Once he had spoken to her family about me, they changed their minds. "It seems that this boy is also a skilled trader. He can join us in the cloth shop," they decided. So they fixed the wedding between us.

Each side had to meet its share of the wedding expenses. The family of the groom had to contribute jewelry on his behalf, and the family of the bride would do the same. We had a gold chain made for the *thirumangalyam*, the marital necklace that she would wear. At the time, one sovereign, eight grams of gold, cost less than fifty rupees. We bought five sovereigns of gold to make that necklace, and beyond that, we spent another hundred rupees. From Chellammal's side, they gave twenty sovereigns of gold jewelry for the bride to wear on her neck, ears, and arms. Then as now, the family of the bride had to give much more than the family of the groom did.

The wedding was held at home. Two or three of Appa's relatives came as guests from somewhere else, but that was all. Most people wouldn't even print wedding invitations in those days. Those with money might do this, but we were poor. The wedding guests were fed three times. Rice, sambar, *rasam*, pickles, eggplant, beans or ridge gourds: these were the things that made a wedding feast back then. In the houses of the rich, there would also be a *payasam* for dessert. For the poor, there was nothing sweet to eat.

The wedding feast, with freshly cooked rice and everything else, was served on the first afternoon of the wedding. That night, we ate what was left over from the afternoon, and what remained of this food was covered with water so it wouldn't spoil. The next morning, the guests were given that old rice to eat once more. But no one took this the wrong way. After all, we had fed them with rice, which was itself enough of an honor for a wedding. Rice wasn't all that easily available back then. It would have to come by ship from Burma—where were the paddy fields in that dry village? *Kambu, keppai,* everyone usually lived on such millets.

There were a few rituals that were conducted according to the customs of those times: circling the ritual implements together, stepping onto a grinding stone, exchanging garlands, things like that. But there was no Brahmin priest to officiate the wedding. To do this would have cost more money, and so instead of a Brahmin, some of the most respected people in the village conducted the wedding. That was how things were often done at the time.

There was another custom that people would follow in those days, once a wedding was over. The bride's family was expected to feed the groom for the first three months after the wedding. This practice was called *mappillai chooru,* "food for the groom." As the groom, I lived with Chellammal's family for those first three months, and when that time had passed, we came back to my family's house in the village.

Around the same time, a wedding was also fixed for one of my younger brothers. My older brothers approached me to say that they needed some jewelry for his marriage. "We don't have anything in hand; just give us what we had given you," they told me. They took back that gold chain, putting my wife's *thali,* her marital ornament, on some yellow cord for her to wear. When it came to weddings in the family, you couldn't refuse to do such things. I don't think Chellammal was angry about this, and no one in her family complained.

Before the wedding, we weren't allowed to talk to each other. They wouldn't even let us see each other's faces. I didn't see her face at all on our first night together. Everything happened in the dark that night, and I saw her only the next morning.

Obviously, I was nervous that night. I'd never done such things with anyone in Burma. I may have had those desires, but I never had the experience. There used to be a book called the *Kokkokam,* where you could learn about such things.[2] You could get it in bookstores, but over time, it became difficult to find such books. I had heard about the *Kokkokam,* but no one gave me anything like it after the wedding. I've never had the chance to look at a copy myself.

During the first few years of our marriage, the two of us never fought. Chellammal was very caring with me and always respectful. She woke up every morning before I did. For some time, she insisted on touching my feet to pay her respects before getting up each morning. That's how much deference she showed at first.

No wife in India would call her husband by name. *Yeenga,* that's how she addressed me—the word doesn't mean anything, but it's a respectful way of calling someone. I never got used to calling her by name, either. But if I said "Hey!" to call her, or anything else as casual as that, she might come after me—"What, call me 'hey,' will you?" she'd shout.

*Yeendi,* "Hey, woman!" was also something I couldn't say, something she also found disrespectful. Chellammal was born in a wealthier family, while we were poor and struggling. I had to give her what she was due. I always treated her with respect, whenever I spoke to her, and she also spoke respectfully to me.

We did fight, of course. Those days, husbands tormented their wives. That was an era in which men treated women as their slaves. They would beat them, or come home drunk and rip the wedding ornaments from their necks. Women were expected always to wake up before their husbands and to sleep only after their husbands had slept. They would have to touch their husband's feet to pay their respects. Women were forced to do such things.

When Chellammal and I fought, I could never hit her. I never wanted to, but even if I did, she would have hit me right back, that's how daring she was. If I scolded her, she would scold me. "Hey, donkey!" I'd say. "Enough of this donkey talk, horse talk!" she'd shout back. There was nothing to do but to put up with all this. I couldn't question what she said.

In spite of this all, there is love only where there are quarrels. These two things, love and war, always come together. When people love in vain, they go their own ways. But Chellammal and I, though we often fought, never hated each other for this. How could we have had eight children, if that love hadn't been there between us?

Two of our children, Ganesan and Rupavathi, were born when we were still in Pudur. Ganesan, our first, was born on a jute sack in the house of Chellammal's parents. They had her lie down on some hay that they had spread out on the floor. I was waiting outside the house.

Then, when he was born, Chellammal's mother came out to tell me. "He looks like you," she said. Because her daughter was bleeding from the delivery, we took her to see a doctor in Nagalapuram. The doctor told her to take some whiskey for the pain and sent me to the town of Virudhunagar to buy a bottle.

When Ganesan was born, I had no one around to share the joy of his birth. I was the only one among my family still in Pudur. Everyone else had gone in other directions. My brother Shanmugam had gone off to tend a shop of his own. Gurusamy was doing business in Madurai. Mutharasu had already gone to Chennai, and my youngest brother, Raja, was also there, working in another shop for a wage. I had no one aside from my wife in Pudur. Her family was even happier at Ganesan's birth than I was—they had no sons at all in that family.

Soon after coming back to Pudur from Burma, I opened a small provisions shop in the village. That shop lasted for just three months after I got married. I didn't have the money to keep it stocked with goods when they ran out. I could have taken out loans, but they would have to be repaid. In Burma, things were different: the dealers kept lending us goods on credit, and we could keep doing business with what they gave us. There, we had more income and spent much less. Here, I earned much less, and there were many more expenses to handle.

Around that time, the boy who was working in my father-in-law's cloth shop left for another shop. He was angry that Mama's daughter hadn't been given to him in marriage, and so he decided to compete against the business.[3] Whenever the usual customers would leave the shop with their purchases in hand, he would stop them on the road. "I've left that shop and joined this one now," he'd say. He would even beg them: "Next time you come, please visit our shop instead of that one." That was the kind of person he was.

There was no one now to help out at Mama's shop, so he decided to keep me beside him. I had joined their house as a son-in-law, but they had only two daughters in the family, no sons. "Once we're gone, who else will get everything but our son-in-law?" he and his brother must have asked themselves. "One day, he and his wife will inherit everything we have. Why not ask him to look after the shop now?"

To be frank, Mama and his elder brother kept me in that shop like a peon. There was no respect for what I did for them, but even so, I had to endure what came and to look after that shop as best I could. For four years, I worked in that cloth shop as their assistant. Though I had a family of my own and two children, they paid me just twenty-two rupees each month for our expenses. This was what we lived on.

We could eat with those rupees, but that was all. Whatever groceries we needed, I would buy on credit from another provisions shop. Then, each month when I was paid, I would take all the money and give it to that shop owner. There was never a single cent left over. We couldn't buy anything else. If there was some expense that had to be met, I would have to go to Mama and ask him for money, explaining what we needed. We could never buy something just because we wanted it. I couldn't buy anything for my own wife—not even some jasmine flowers to pin in her hair. This was how we had to live at the time.

Her family had a milch cow, and they brought us a little milk every day. Each morning, we boiled some of that milk with a bit of palm sugar and coffee powder to drink. For a quarter of an anna, we could buy enough coffee powder to last four days. We ate whatever Chellammal cooked in the afternoon and then the same thing again at night. We poured water over what was left each night and ate that soured water and gruel the next morning, with some salt and a raw green pepper for taste. With that breakfast and a little coffee, I'd go off to work.

There was *rasam* to flavor the grain we ate each afternoon but nothing more than that. No lentils or any vegetables; we couldn't afford them. Once in a while, for a quarter of an anna, I would buy a fried *vadai* to eat.[4] Every now and then, we could have rice, but we mostly ate boiled millets and whatever other grains came from my brother's field.

Two or three times a month, Mama's elder brother, Shanmugavel Nadar, would offer us a meal. He and his brother often took our children to their house to raise for some time. There were no other children in that house, no other heirs but these, and so they looked after some of the expenses of our children. They would panic if these two ever got sick or felt even a little ill. I was the father, but those men were much more careful with them than I was.

11

There are photographs meant to capture some moment as it is. Others do something very different—they sketch a life yet to come. That's what this portrait of Ayya and Paati must have been: a pair of figures mounted high upon a wall within every house they kept, calmly taking in the domestic struggles occurring below, reminding my grandparents of a comfort and peace that might still fall within their reach. An image not of a moment but of its longings.

Ayya still remembers that day at Victoria Studio. The studio was on a small lane near the Meenakshi temple in Madurai. It was full of things that gave the impression of wealth and leisure: costume jewelry, toys, books, carved wooden furniture, porcelain ceramics—things, that is, generally missing from the lives of those who posed here for pictures. The photographer and his assistants would arrange their subjects among these foreign objects, demanding postures of bluffed repose. "Wear this . . . Hold that . . . Stand like this . . . Bend your arms like that . . ."

This portrait, in other words, presents much more than the private world of an individual household. This is domestic life as national theater, an image of the progress to be made, atom by atom, conjugal nucleus by nucleus. Paati, standing at attention beside her husband, has an essential role to play in the drama of national development. She is pregnant, expecting another child. But she looks tired already, arms dangling loosely from the puffed sleeves of her blouse.

Marriage appears here as a relation between two people: a woman and a man. We know, though, that their wedding had pulled together families much larger than this pair. Paati and Ayya are "cross-cousins": in the infinite extension of Dravidian kin relations, one is the daughter of the other's father's cousin-sister. These families are deeply implicated in the emotional texture of their marriage, although how, these faces do not say.

Beside Paati, Ayya's face looks plump and well fed. The photographers had lent him a suit coat and shoes. The sleeves of the coat were fraying, and the shoes had holes in them, but none of this is visible in the photograph they took. Ayya's brother Gurusamy had given him the watch on his wrist. My grandfather couldn't afford yet to buy one on his own.

Unlike most Tamil men, Ayya has no mustache on his face. Coming of age in Burma, he never let this hair grow out. Like most of his Burmese friends, he had used a pair of quarter-anna coins to pluck out each of the hairs above his lips until they stopped growing altogether. Sometimes, back in India, people who didn't know him would ask if he was a Brahmin.

To me, both Ayya and Paati look proud in the photograph. Though she is standing while he sits, they both seem to be doing much more than acting out a show of domestic servitude. Look at the buoyant cut of her blouse and the jaunty angles of his collar, the serenity of their eyes and the confidence in their distance from each other. They seem to be looking through, seeing past, the charade of the studio portrait. They may not see all that the twentieth century has in store for them, but there is strength in their grasp of a future already on its way.

⌇

# DEALING CLOTH IN A TIME OF WAR

# 12

PUDUR WAS JUST A SMALL VILLAGE, PART OF THE ETTAIYAPURAM zamindari estate.[1] Because the zamindar himself had died, his mother looked after the affairs of the estate. She had an accountant responsible for collecting taxes from the people who lived there. Pudur's lands belonged to the zamindar, not to the British government. Even when we bought land there in our own names, we had to pay a land tax to the zamindar's people.

Close to Pudur was a small town called Nagalapuram. A weekly market took place there every Thursday. Each week, farmers from all the surrounding villages would bundle up their crops in sacks, loading them onto bullock carts to sell. Traders from all those villages would also travel there on bullock carts, bringing their goods to the Thursday market. They would sell what they had and take back what they earned, or use the money to buy what they needed themselves. All the biggest traders at that market were Nadars by caste.

Pudur also had a small weekly market, in the *pettai* marketplace just outside the village. Four or five bullock carts would come from the south, bringing crops that grew in that area. Sugarcane grew well on that side of the village. There were many coconut groves, and the owners of those groves would load their carts with coconuts to sell. They would bring *nongu*, palmyra fruit, from the trees that grew on the surrounding lands. One *nongu* cost just a quarter of an anna back then. They were good to eat, with a fresh, cool taste, though the skin of the *nongu* was always a little astringent. You could peel off the skin if you wanted, or eat them as they came.

The bazaar in Pudur was close to that *pettai* and also close to the Nadar school—after all, it was just a small village. There used to be many stores in that bazaar, small shops of different kinds: provisions stores where you could buy all kinds of things to cook and eat, a stationery shop, a stall that sold betel nut, one that sold vegetables, another that sold roasted gram. Mama's cloth shop was also located in that bazaar.

None of those stores exist now. They all closed their doors a long time ago, and everyone went to the city or somewhere else to seek out a livelihood. These days, that village is empty.

When I began working at the cloth shop, business was poor. That trade ran completely on credit. There was no way around it—those who bought our goods never had money to give. It hadn't rained very much at the time, and people were hungry.

It was also wartime. Because the cloth trade was under government control, it was difficult to do business. The mills weren't making very much cloth or fabric. There was no electricity, no transport, no cars or trucks to go from one place to another. You couldn't move goods around very easily. Those bundles of cloth, we often had to carry them on our heads from place to place instead of loading them onto bullock carts. It was that kind of time.

Then there were the government restrictions on the sale of cloth. Because of these controls, mills weren't willing to give us their goods. The government would fix a seal onto each bundle of cloth, ordering the mills to sell those bundles at an official price, a fixed rate. But then the mill owners devised a plan in response. They would hide away most of their cloth and sell what was left at twice the price, refusing to give out anything else.

These were the circumstances of the cloth trade at the time. It was difficult to get ahold of these goods, and we struggled to collect on what we sold. The government would ration out limited amounts of cloth to us: "You've been allotted this many barrels. You've got to go to such-and-such place to get them," they would tell us. And so we would go and wait to take whatever they were willing to give us there.

Wherever they told us to go, we had to reach on foot. And because we never bought that much cloth at a time, we couldn't afford to hire anyone else to carry it for us. I've walked fifteen miles, from village to village, carrying those bundles of cloth. I would lift them onto my own head to bring back to Pudur. Everyone was doing this at the time. I had no choice. I did the same.

In those days, all the stores selling goods in the village would put up a sheet in the front to block sunlight from coming into the shop. Because of this practice, in the cloth shop, no one could really see the color of the fabric. Most of what we stocked were fabrics that would bleed their dyes. So what they would do, my father-in-law and his brother, was to hide this cloth from the light and lie to the customers in order to sell it.

There was good handloomed cloth available then, dyed with colors that wouldn't bleed. There were many weavers with their own handlooms in the villages nearby. They'd weave their own cloth and bring it to the shops to sell to merchants like Mama. Because this was good cloth that they had made carefully, it was a little expensive to buy. "Give us something for a lower price," the cloth traders would always say. And so the weavers would bring them poorer and cheaper clothes and saris that would bleed their colors.

When the weavers came with such inferior cloth to sell, we would bargain with them for a lesser price. We never paid the price they asked for but kept bargaining instead, for a long time, to bring that price down. Mama was always the one who spoke to them. He tried to make me do the same thing, to tell the same lies, but I never learned to lie like he did.

There was always an invoice to fill out when goods were sold. In Mama's shop, they had a way of showing that invoice deceitfully to their customers. The proper invoice for what was sold would remain on top, and underneath was the invoice for another sale. One amount was written on the top sheet, another amount on the sheet below. The amount written below would be much higher, and this is what they would show their customers: "See, here's the price we're selling it for." The farmers would never know how to judge such things.

This was how they sold things in that shop, by tricking people. Those days, it was mostly farmers who came to buy cloth from us. When the shopkeepers sold goods to farmers, they would always sell on credit, another reason why they would use such tricks. The farmers who came to the store were good and honest people—they had land but never enough income to meet their expenses. A wedding, a death in the family, whenever such things happened, they'd have to buy cloth on credit to fulfill their responsibilities.

The farmers would come to the shop, expecting they could get what they needed on credit. They'd never be able to repay these debts within a week or ten days, and so the shopkeepers would send them away. "Come back with someone trustworthy who's willing to guarantee the loan," they'd say. "We can't give the goods in your name, but we can write out the debt in his name."

If a month had passed and the farmer still hadn't paid for the cloth, they'd begin to collect interest, beginning with the original date of the sale. Interest in those days was collected at the rate of two on every hundred per month. Mama and his brother would always collect all of this interest, even if just a few days had passed beyond that one month.

The shop was just a small room, nothing more, covered with that sheet in front so that it was very dark inside. The customers would have to bring the cloth out into the sunlight to tell the difference between good fabric and bad. But who would dare do this, these poor people buying from them on credit? This was how Mama managed to fool them.

"Will this dye fade?" the customers would ask. "It'll never fade!" the shopkeeper would reply, enthusiastically. "Just believe what I say. If the colors bleed, you can bring it back to me."

Mama would never try to trick customers who lived in Pudur. If they bought something from him that faded easily, they'd never come back to the shop again. It was generally those who came from nearly villages who were duped at the shop.

They would come by bullock cart, from eight or ten kilometers away. They would come and complain very sadly about something they'd bought from him before: "Look, sir. All the dye bled away from the cloth that I bought from you."

He'd say something right away: "Really? But that never happens with this cloth; it never fades like that." Then, it would seem as though he was thinking more about this problem.

"I know," he'd say after some time. "You must have taken those clothes to be cleaned by the washerman, and he probably put them at the bottom of his pile, where there was too much steam. That's probably why they faded."

This was how Mama handled such situations. "If you wash these clothes in hot water, and expose them to too much steam, of course their colors will bleed. The washerman must have heated them up too much. What can I do if he goes and does something like that?"

These were the kinds of tricks he used. I didn't like any of this, and I didn't know how to lie like he did. I worked in that cloth shop for about four or five years, but I never cared about the work I was doing there. Mama and his brother kept me there like a servant, that was all: "Go get this and come . . . Do that . . . Do this . . . Hold this . . . Take that . . ."

This was how they made me work all those years. There was a milch cow at their house, and sometimes they'd even ask me to bathe and clean that cow. I could never refuse, even when they told me to do such things.

My brother Gurusamy was already in Madurai at that time. I was still working in the shop in Pudur, but the business was going poorly. I couldn't go back to Burma. And now that I had two children, there wasn't enough business to support all of us. Meanwhile, Gurusamy's trade in Madurai was growing, and he needed someone to help him. "My younger brother is a good trader," he thought to himself. "It would be useful to have him here with me."

Gurusamy had sold what jewelry they had and raised a little money for his business in Madurai. At first, he was dealing in rice, but he couldn't handle that trade very well. Then, he opened up a small fruit stall, but that also went poorly. Finally, I helped him find a house and storefront in the East Napalam area of Madurai. Sweet limes and oranges were selling well at the time, and he began dealing in these fruits as a wholesale trader. Eventually, things began to go well for him, so well that he needed someone else with him to keep up.

Back in Pudur, the cloth shop was failing. Chellammal and I could barely live on what her father and uncle paid us for our expenses, that was how bad things were. "It isn't right to stay here any longer," I thought to myself. "We have children. We need to raise them somehow. We need to feed them, send them to school. Unless I go somewhere else to work, there won't be enough to do all this." And so, when Gurusamy called on me, we went right away to Madurai.

"I'm going to Madurai to help out my brother," I went and said to Mama.

"Fine, go," he replied. And there wasn't a single thing he gave us when we left. He could have given us just ten or twenty rupees. "Go do business with your brother, I want you to do well," he could have said. But he didn't say such things, nor did he seem angry that I wanted to leave. "If he wants to go, let him go"—that's how little he seemed to care about my leaving.

The reason was simply this. Mama and his brother didn't need anyone else to help out at their shop anymore. There was hardly any business left, and they could handle what there was on their own. That's how things were—not just for them but for everyone in the village at that time.

Back when I was still in Burma, I had a friend named Sathappa Pillai. He was a reporter for a Tamil newspaper there, the *Rasigar*

*Ranjani,* which was published once a week from Rangoon. I tried to help him out at times, telling him when anything important happened in Okpo. Because he was a reporter, and my friend, I knew all about the Indian independence struggle and the acts of resistance against British rule that were taking place in India. I even knew when Nehru came to visit Rangoon with his daughter, Indira Gandhi.

Once, while we were still living in Pudur, Gandhi came to speak in Madurai. It must have been 1945 or 1946. Everyone went from Pudur to see him, and I also went along with them, to hear Gandhi speak. He was talking at the racecourse in Madurai, and a huge crowd had gathered. There was a microphone on the stage, but because the British refused to supply the event with electricity, it didn't work. Gandhi spoke for some time without a microphone, and those who could hear him listened. Where we were standing, we couldn't hear anything. We watched what was happening on that stage, and then we came back home.

At the time, there was no freedom of the press in India. Write the wrong thing, and the British would throw you in jail. Even when India got its independence one day in 1947, I didn't know this had happened. I didn't know what had happened that day. I wasn't reading the papers at the time, and no one told me anything about this event.

I was already in Madurai then. That day, like every other day, I spent doing business. Ten days later, I found out about India's independence.

∽

# DINDIGUL, 1951

# 13

Yes, Indian independence—something else from those years to ponder. But wait a minute. What did he just say? Ten days later? Could he be mistaken? This event that supposedly led an entire country to convulse with joy at the stroke of midnight, how could it have passed unnoticed by my grandfather for so long? This might be less puzzling if Ayya was in a distant and out-of-the-way place, beyond the reach of radios and newspapers. But he says that he was already living and working in Madurai, a city of over 300,000 people at the time, a place that Gandhi himself had addressed several times over the many decades of the independence movement. How could Ayya have missed the very culmination of this struggle?

The look and feel of social phenomena like nationalism depend entirely on where one is looking from. In the years that led up to the moment of India's independence from Britain, Ayya and his father-in-law were dealing in one of the central symbols of this struggle: handloomed Indian cloth. For nationalist leaders, handloomed cloth was one of the most visible markers of what was at stake in the freedom struggle, the very possibility of making a living in the world without multiplying debts to the industrial mills of Manchester and Lancaster. But for these traders, in villages like Pudur, the same cloth was itself a tool of division and exploitation—a symbol less of letting go than holding tight.

A few years after Ayya came to Madurai, his father-in-law, Chinnathambi Nadar, asked him to purchase an iron safe for the cloth shop and send it back to Pudur. Iron safes were manufactured and sold at the time in Dindigul, an industrial town north of Madurai. In Dindigul, Ayya chose two safes made by Luxmi & Co. Safe Manufacturers—one for his father-in-law and another for his youngest brother, Raja, in Madras.

The dark green safe was a double-door model, very heavy, Ayya recalls. He arranged to have it inscribed in both Tamil and English with the name of Animuthu Nadar, Chinnathambi Nadar's other son-in-law and Ayya's "co-brother," married to Paati's sister. Scenes from a tropical beach and other colorful details were painted onto the front, and its sides were painted with landscapes of trees and flowers. Ayya paid more than a thousand rupees for the safe.

At the time, there were no banks in the village of Pudur, and merchants kept their money locked up within their own shops. Chinnathambi Nadar would keep the key to the safe on a thick silver chain with wide hoops of equal diameter fastened onto both of its ends. Instead of a shirt on his torso, Chinnathambi Nadar wore this chain, strolling around the village with its length thrown over his shoulder and the key tucked into his waist.

At the end of each day, Chinnathambi Nadar carefully added up all the money left in the safe. The handles on its doors were constructed in the shape of clenched metal hands. To reach his money, the man would have wrapped his own hands around these metal fists. I imagine this gesture as a reminder of the relationships through which everything here was earned or, more darkly, of the truth that whatever they earned was taken out of the hands of others.

The double-door model by Luxmi & Co. remains in a dusty corner of Animuthu Nadar's old house in Pudur. He is gone, as is his wife, and most of his children have left Pudur. His youngest son, who looks after a small orchard on the edge of the village, now keeps sacks of onions and chilies heaped up around the safe. In the bazaar, the cloth store is long gone, and it seems that someone is renting out that room now to store sacks of fertilizer.

༼ঌ

# A FOOTHOLD IN MADURAI

# 14

POTS, PLATES, WE HAD NO SUCH THINGS WHEN WE WENT TO
Madurai. I had two *veshtis* and a couple of shirts and vests.[1] Chellammal had two or three saris and blouses, the children too a couple
of things to wear. Beyond this, we took little with us. Whatever we
did have, we left behind in Pudur. Gurusamy's family was already
in Madurai, and when we arrived there, we planned to live and eat
together, as a joint family.

East Napalam was a small lane near East Masi Street, in the
middle of the town. My brother's house and shop were side by side
on that lane. We stayed with them for the first three months, but
Chellammal didn't like this at all.

Gurusamy's wife was ill with what they called "hysteria." She used
to love to eat duck curry. She would go to the market to buy some
duck and cook it for herself. She'd give us a small bit of what she
made, then hide away the rest to eat by herself.

My wife didn't like this, and she made it known. Then Gurusamy's
wife would say, "You've come into my house to insist on this and

that?" This was also something that Chellammal didn't like. "Let's look for somewhere else to live," she said. And so we went.

My brother had a fruit business. The business worked on a commission basis. Brokers and farmers sent him their fruit, and he took a 10 percent commission on whatever he could sell. Sweet limes were selling very well in those days, as doctors encouraged their patients to eat the fruit. Sweet limes didn't grow anywhere near Madurai and would come from Andhra Pradesh. We would sell them to fruit stall vendors and collect what they owed us. We did so well that some of the biggest traders in Madurai began to give us their fruit on commission. We would always sell their goods quickly and made sure that payments were made promptly. Many others began to send us their oranges, grapes, and other fruit.

When these goods came to the shop by truck, I was always there to receive them and to sell them off. My brother wasn't very interested in being a trader. He liked to chew betel nut: he would chew half a pack just like that, all at once.[2] Sitting on the steps of his shop, he'd chew on that betel nut, spit what came out, and keep on talking with his friends. The whole day would pass like this—a day's work for him.

Everything else, I would do. Selling the fruit that came, paying out and collecting money, I looked after all these things. The shop was known by his name, Gurusamy Nadar, and all the business was conducted in his name. But no one who sent us goods knew who this Gurusamy Nadar was. Everyone thought that I was him. That was how things went.

We did well. No matter how much they sent us, we managed to sell it, and we always paid promptly for whatever we sold. My brother believed in me. It was enough for him that I was involved. If someone ever complained, he would point me out: "He's the one doing all the work. Go ask him what happened." He would never question what I did.

At first, everything about this fruit business was new to me. I had run a provisions store in Burma and then worked in a cloth shop in

Pudur. Still, I managed to learn this trade quite easily. Everything here was wholesale, and what I had to do was to sell all the fruit off, basket by basket. Back then, nothing was accounted for by weight. I had to count each fruit, one by one, setting aside any bad fruit that I found as I was counting. After some time, once I'd gotten used to doing this, I was able to add up those numbers very quickly.

A truckload of sweet limes would come loosely packed, as a huge pile of fruit. There was no packaging: the limes were just plucked from the trees and loaded onto the trucks. All that fruit had to be counted out and kept in the shop. I had to separate the fruit into three different kinds: larger ones, smaller ones, and fruit that was already going bad. I would remove the rotten ones and sell what was still good.

Later, I had to account for everything with my brother: how much we sold the larger ones for, the price at which the smaller ones sold, and what we got for selling off the bad ones too. How many thousands of each kind we received, how much these thousands had sold for, all such things I described to Gurusamy each day.

Because arithmetic came so easily to me, I could make those calculations quickly and correctly when I told him how we'd done each day. My memory was strong back then. Each day, for example, we would have to pay our fruit sellers what we owed them. I could say how much we owed each of them without even looking at my account books. I could repeat these details from memory because they had been recorded so firmly in my mind. All of this I could recall instantly in those days: how much of a balance remained on this person's account, how much we had collected from them yesterday, how much they'd paid today, and how much more they still owed after having paid this much yesterday and today.

The computers that we have these days are also brains, in a sense; people rely now on the assistance of these computer-brains. Back then, I never had a computer to help me think. I knew nothing about the existence of such machines. But my own brain worked quite well, and it would preserve the details of all those accounts and numbers, all those balances, day by day.

This is what we call *vay kanakku,* "spoken accounts." Each night, as I was lying down, I would retell all those debts and payments to myself: how much we owed someone, and how much he owed us. No one taught me how to do this, but somehow, I began to commit these accounts to memory on my own.

Buyers would rarely pay us in cash for what we sold them. They bought on credit, and we always had to record what they owed us before giving them anything more. The buyers would have to take our fruit and then sell it themselves so that they could repay us. Suppose someone bought some fruit for fifty rupees. On the first day, they might be able to pay back only thirty rupees. A balance of twenty rupees would remain the next morning, and once again, we'd have to give them more fruit. Now, they would take this to sell as well.

All of this, I would remember: I could say how much of a balance remained after the first day, how much they paid back the next day, and how much remained unpaid. At the time, we were doing business like this with about thirty different people, each with their own accounts, their own balances to remember. If I ever forgot anything, the ledgers were always there to look at.

This was a trade that I really enjoyed. I wasn't that involved in the cloth trade. There were all the lies that my father-in-law and his brother would tell, but here, we couldn't lie like that. I might give someone some fruit, promising that it was good. Suppose they looked it over and said that it looked bad: I would have to take it back and give them something else. Why would they take something that was already rotten? If it looked bad to them, I had to exchange it right there.

Some people would take our fruit without paying us back for a long time, sometimes even for a year or more. For such people, who kept their balances unpaid for so long, we raised our prices by five rupees. Those who paid us back in regular installments got a lower price. All such things we had to keep secret: who got what price, the price for those who bought on credit, the price for those who bought with cash, and so on.

These were the tricks we had to use. And there was nothing wrong in that. Each day we lost money to those who bought from us on credit, though they would sell that fruit immediately and make something for themselves. With these buyers, we were always taking a risk. This is why we raised their prices. Even the invoices would show a lower price than what we gave them.

Those days I used to get up at five each morning. As soon as I woke up, I'd have some rice gruel or something else, then go straight to the shop. The shop was very close to where we lived, just half a kilometer away. Sometimes I would walk. Otherwise, I would take the bicycle. By cycle, it took less than ten minutes to get there.

By the time I got to the shop, around 5:30, they would already be unloading the fruit from the trucks, and our buyers would also be waiting to take what they needed. Right away, we would begin to trade, and we would continue until there was no more fruit to sell or until there was no one else left to buy what we still had. Each day, I would be home in time for lunch; after two in the afternoon, there was never any business.

Every afternoon, I took home as much fruit as the children needed. They were never there when I came home—at that hour, everyone was at school. I would eat, and then I might lie down for some rest. After half an hour, I would go back to the shop once again. Now it was time to do the accounts: to record how much we'd given and to whom, who'd paid us that day, who still owed us money, and how much they owed. Then, in the evenings, I would walk around for a couple of hours, collecting what our buyers owed us. By the time I came back to the house, the children were already asleep.

I knew nothing about raising these children, nor did I think at all about how to raise them. Encouraging them to study, taking them to school, Chellammal looked after all such things. Did the children have some expense that needed to be met? "What's the expense? How much do you need? Here, I've got some money," I'd say. Were there school fees to be paid? "Here, take this," I'd tell them and arrange for whatever money they needed. Only when they were on leave from school did I have the chance to see them or spend time with them at all.

Seven days each week, I had to work—that was how it went. Once in a while, there was a break in what we were doing, with no one around to buy or sell anything. When that happened, I would take the bicycle home, taking along something for the children. "Ayya's come, Ayya's come! Has he brought anything for us?" they would ask each other, happily. They would come to me, and we would play for awhile before I had to go back to the shop again.

Sometimes, in the evenings, after I finished my accounts, I would cycle home for a quick visit. Even then, I could stay for just fifteen minutes, that was all.

Not once did Chellammal ever come to the shop. When I came home especially late, she would ask what took me so long. "What, was there a big crowd at the shop, is that why you've been gone all this time?" She knew how to cook and raise the children, but she knew nothing about the business. She would often argue with me about money: "Look at how little you've given me! Who else are you earning all of this for?"

For twelve years, I worked in that shop with my elder brother. All the rest of our children were born in those years. Just like that, they seemed to appear, one after another every two years. Chellammal was pregnant with Murugesan when we came to Madurai. Then, we had five more children here.

Birth control wasn't something we practiced back then. We hardly knew anything about such matters. Each time we had another child, the doctor would talk to us about these techniques. Sometimes, we even tried to do what he suggested. But it didn't work. Both Kannan and Meena were born in spite of those efforts.

This is how things were in those days. Now they stop with one child, or two. Some people never even have children. But back then, men and women would have seven or eight children. All of my siblings, for example, had seven or eight. Then there were those who had ten, twelve, even fifteen of them!

Once, when Chellammal was pregnant once again, we went to the hospital for an abortion. After that she would get anxious whenever I came close to her. From that time on, she made sure that we kept our distance from each other. My wife, married at the age of fifteen, with eight children by the age of thirty-two . . .

∾

GOPAL STUDIO, 1953

# 15

Ganesan and Rupavathi are wearing new clothes. Paati bought them for the Diwali festival just a few days back. The photographer has slipped a ring onto the boy's finger and given the girl a handbag to hold. It's very hot and bright under the studio lights, as the children wait for the man ducked under the cloth behind his camera.

Rupavathi is eight years old, Ganesan ten. They often fight. She helps her mother with the cooking, setting out and washing the plates, sweeping and washing the floor. Ganesan draws water from the well each morning, buys groceries, and walks the younger kids to school and to the doctor for ointments and shots. They hardly see Ayya, always at the shop.

Born in the village of Pudur, the children and their parents came by bus to the city of Madurai in 1947. They were part of a massive wave of migrants who swelled the population of Tamil Nadu's cities and towns in the 1940s, more so than in any other decade of the twentieth century. Now these children, like their parents, have to take their experience of the city as a means of education: whom to count as friends, how to keep track of their things.

Urban migration is often imagined as a straightforward phenomenon, a movement from country to city in search of new opportunities for growth and development. But rural life has always been more dynamic than this. People have been moving in and out of Indian villages for centuries, taking advantage of various chances to work, travel, and trade. Think of Ayya and his Burmese sojourn. Or of what Ganesan himself has been doing in the last few years.

Ganesan walks each morning now to the Madurai Virudhunagar Nadar Higher Primary School nearby. But for the previous two years, he had been studying back in Pudur. Paati's uncle Shanmugavel Nadar was still childless, and he had wanted Ganesan to settle in the village as his own heir. Ayya and Paati did their best to try to respect these wishes.

In Pudur, Ganesan liked wandering through the fields, eating roasted millets with curd, jumping into a well each day to bathe. He always ran around barefoot. Once, when he was seven, he noticed there were ulcers on his heels. Ayya came to see him with a packet of Lifebuoy soap. He washed off the boy's feet and bought him a pair of slippers, the first he'd had.

Ganesan liked Pudur, but there were many things he missed in Madurai: the wooden rocking horse at home, the Ovaltine that all the children drank, and the Woodwards Gripe Water, which his mother had bought for the babies but the older children would sip secretly themselves. Then there was all the fruit that came from his father's shop: mangoes, oranges, tangerines, grapes, figs, jujubas, pomegranates, apples, always changing with the seasons.

The boy made excuses to come back to Madurai from Pudur. When he began to wear glasses, he lied and said that he had to go and get them changed in the city. Shanmugavel Nadar insisted that Ganesan stay in the village. But Chinnathambi Nadar, the boy's grandfather, pulled him aside. "Whatever you want to do, just do that," he told him.

Back in Madurai now, Ganesan is in the sixth grade. The tennis racket in his hands is also from the studio. In the evenings, he and the other children kick balls and run around the narrow urban lane where they live. They fly kites, play hide and seek. Mothers on the lane look after all the kids that run past their doorways—wherever they came from, wherever they're going.

∽

# A SHOP OF MY OWN

# 16

TAKE A SMALL GRAIN OF SAND. THINK OF THE MOUNTAIN THAT IT comes from. Slowly pushed along by rainwater, farther and farther down, until at last it reaches the sea. Some of that sand sometimes remains along the edge of a river. Take some of it. Think about how useful this sand can be, heaped up along both banks of that river.

Whatever trade you take up, it's always best to begin small then slowly grow. Some try to grow too quickly and stumble, losing everything they had at the start. So many companies have failed like this. They begin with a big establishment, hiring a hundred workers from the start. Machines must be bought; laborers must be managed. But for 1,000 rupees in expenses, what they produce is worth only 500 rupees. Then, to try to sell more, they drop their prices by half. Still, they can't sell enough. What will they do?

My business was never that big. When I began a shop of my own, I invested just 3,000 rupees. With just that much capital, I raised eight children and educated them all. How much would I have earned, how much would I have spent? How many things would I have bought? Like those small grains of sand, I accumulated all of this bit by bit, one anna at a time.

I was already forty years old when I started my own business, when I opened the shop in the last month of 1959. I was working till then for someone else, although it wasn't exactly a salary that I was paid. Gurusamy would give us whatever we needed for our expenses. I would take what we needed for the house, for the children, and note the amount on our ledgers.

Around that time, Gurusamy's business began to falter. He bought a house and had much less money on hand. He took out loans. Our brother Mutharasu sent some money back from Burma, but even this he couldn't repay. There wasn't enough to pay those who had sent their goods to the shop. Without our payments, would they keep sending their fruit? The business began to decline.

"In spite of all this, I've still got to pay Mariappan," my brother thought. "Maybe he ought to split off and begin a business of his own. Then at least I'd have fewer expenses to worry about."

We also had many children of our own, and I was worried about our expenses, about whether we'd be able to educate them all. I had managed to save a small amount each month from what my brother gave me. With this money, I established my own shop.

As soon as I opened this shop, Gurusamy's business foundered even more. He didn't know very much about the trade to begin with: he didn't have the interest or the practice. His son had earned a bachelor of commerce degree. In those days, everyone thought of that as a very good degree. You could easily get government work or a job at the State Bank of India; put in an application, and they'd take you right away. But that boy refused to look for such jobs. "I won't work as a servant for anyone else. I don't want to listen to what others tell me I ought to do. I will work for myself, and nothing else," he declared, and came to look after Gurusamy's shop. But what could he know about the fruit trade?

People would ask him for goods on credit, offering to pay five rupees more per basket. Without even thinking twice, he would give them what they wanted, but he would never get back his money. Then, those who sent their fruit to the shop would ask him for advances: "I've got this much fruit; just give me 1,000 rupees as an advance, and I'll pay off the debt with more fruit," they would tell him. He would give out these advances, but they would take them and never send their goods in exchange. At every turn, he was fooled like this, and Gurusamy's business slowly turned to dust. Eventually, he closed down his shop in Madurai and went off to Madras.

I, meanwhile, had a great deal of confidence in my own abilities. I felt as though I could go anywhere, do anything—I had that kind of courage back then. Everyone in that trade knew something about me. When they heard that I was opening a shop of my own in Madurai, they all began to send their goods straight there. There were many people who admired me at that time. The business went well. Little by little, we began to prosper.

Those with fruit to sell only needed to hear what I had to say, and they would send me as much as I wanted. They searched me out to try to establish a relationship. I didn't need any advertising, which always seemed to me like a wasteful expense. I never even put up a signboard on the wall above my shop. Everyone already knew what they ought to do: send their goods to me, buy their goods from me.

Limes, sweet limes, pineapples, oranges, grapes, I traded in all these things. The limes would come from Dindigul. Pineapples would come from Kodaikanal, and then, when the season had ended there, they would come from Vandi Periyar.[1]

So much came each morning that the shop wasn't big enough to hold all that fruit. Take just the limes: they'd unload truck after truck in front of the shop, and there were 200 to 300 sacks of limes in each of those trucks. At the time, no one else in Madurai received as many limes as I did. All of this had to be sold and turned into money—in those days, a sack of limes for ten rupees. I kept selling off all those sacks myself until, over time, many others began to compete for that trade and eventually took it from me.

Pineapples back then were rare, the harvests very small. For some time, all of Madurai's business in pineapples was mine. Everyone knew that to get good pineapples, you had to go to M. P. M.'s shop. The growers would send that fruit to seven or eight shops: ten baskets to me, five baskets to someone else, and so on. I would buy what came to me as well as what came to all the rest of them. Then I would divide up all those pineapples by grade and sell them off at a price two rupees higher than the market rate. I made a lot of money that way.

They'd send me apples that had been imported into Chennai. Most of these would come from America: apples grew in Kashmir, but this wasn't enough for the market, and so they were sent from America as well. I would also get apples from Australia, as well as grapes and other fruit that was rarely available here. All of this I would also sell on commission.

Every once in a while, we got pomegranates from Kabul. They would first come to Bombay, then to Chennai, and then to Madurai. The fruit was never packed well. They would stow the pomegranates in an open hold when they sent them by ship, tossing just fifty of them into each big basket. With nothing else to cushion them, the fruit would get bruised and crushed along the way. They would begin to rot quickly. But even these, I would find a way to sell.

We depended on nature for our livelihood. I always gave a little fruit to whoever came to buy from me. Back then, one piece of fruit was worth just three or four *paisa*.[2] I'd open it up for the customers. "Break it open and see, taste it and see," I would tell them. Sometimes, I would even taste it with them. Fruit is something that everyone eats, from young children to old men and women. Fruit is good for the body. This is something that everyone knows.

None of my experience in that provisions store or my father-in-law's cloth shop helped with the fruit trade. That was one thing; this was another. At the provisions and cloth stores, we had ever so many different kinds of things to sell, and we had to remember exactly what price to set for each of those things. The fruit business wasn't like that. There were just a few kinds of things at any one time, say, four kinds of fruit. I only had to divide these out by size to price them.

Fresh goods would come each morning. Each night, there was nothing left in the shop. Usually, everything was gone by the afternoon, and I would get a 10 percent commission on whatever we sold that day. Once in a while, things remained unsold, and I would keep whatever lasted for a day or two, to try to sell once more. If anyone approached me later, I would sell that fruit to them.

What could I do if that leftover fruit began to spoil? There were some traders who were willing to buy rotten fruit, and I could sell the old and decaying fruit to them. Nothing was a loss: I always got my commission. After all, these weren't goods that I had paid to buy. I was selling things on behalf of those who had sent them to me. I would take my commission on whatever I sold and give the growers the remainder of the money. That was all there was to it.

Even when things remained unsold, it wasn't a total loss. Sometimes, I would take whatever was left over to some other town to sell off. Those who had sent me that fruit would ask what happened. "No one wanted those goods," I'd tell them. "What can I do? Why did you send me so much in the first place? You could have sent me much less, no?"

After that, of course, they might begin to take their goods to someone else. "Let them go," I'd say to myself. "If not them, someone else will send me their fruit."

Each morning in front of the shop, I would hold small auctions to sell the fruit. There was never any room for anyone to sit down. The buyers would stand there on the road, bidding on what I sold, and I would also stand there with them. I would name a price, and then I could tell, just by looking at someone, whether they were willing to buy at this price or not. I could see whether or not they were thinking of going somewhere else.

If the buyer didn't like the price, they would walk over to another shop to ask about what was for sale there. If the price there was even higher than mine, they wouldn't buy there either. They would wait to see what price they could get their goods for and come back to me only if I offered a price that they could afford.

The fruit buyers used to call me *muthalali*, "boss." Those days, they hardly ever paid cash up front for what they bought. "Fine, just pay me back quickly," I would say, doing whatever I could to quickly clear out whatever fruit I had on hand. I could never collect what they owed me in the shop: I would have to wander around later to wherever they were in order to get that money back. If not the next day, they would pay me on the third day. Sometimes, someone would get away without paying anything at all.

When it comes to business, you can't earn anything without telling lies. All that fruit, for example, I would count out very fast, by fives. I would give a buyer five with one hand, then five with the other, putting these bunches very quickly into the basket, again and again. "Fifty," I would say, but there would only be forty-eight in that basket.

Some of them might come the next day and complain: "There were ten fruit missing from what you gave me yesterday."

"Fine," I'd tell them. "Take these and go."

Someone would buy a sack of fruit from me on credit, for eighty rupees. Someone else would come and offer cash, asking for a rate of seventy rupees. I'd give it to him, quietly, at the rate he wanted— "Don't tell anyone else," I would say. To sell goods worth just seventy rupees for eighty rupees was a trick, of course. But it was only through such ruses that I managed to raise eight children, educate them all, and buy them whatever they needed.

Eventually, I wound up with some money in hand, and I began to lend it out on interest to the other traders. This was how my money really grew. If I had 1,000 rupees, I would lend out 100 or 200 rupees. If I had 10,000, I'd lend out 1,000 or 2,000. I was always very careful about where I lent this money: only to those I dealt with regularly, to those who bought from me, to those who worked at the shop. In those days, you had to sign over some kind of property to borrow money from banks; otherwise you couldn't secure a loan. Other traders would borrow from me to buy their goods, then sell these goods to someone else. I knew that they would get a commission on what they sold.

Each month, I would get 3 percent in interest. But, if I was lending out 1,000 rupees, I would take back 100 immediately and give the borrower only 900 rupees. For the next 100 days, I would collect 10 rupees each day. Then, if 100 days had passed, he would have to pay me another 100 rupees: 100 rupees in interest for the next 100 days. With that, and with the 10 rupees he gave me each day, that 3 percent per month would become more than 5 percent per month. And just like that, the money would begin to swell.

Once, I lent someone 3,000 rupees. He fell at my feet one day, after some time, giving me 500 rupees and crying out, "Ayya, I can't pay you any more."

"Fine, just go," I said, and let it go. People were upset that I'd accepted so little when I let him go. But, over all that time, he must have paid me at least 10,000 rupees for that loan.

As soon as my shop began to do so well, others set up their own shops to compete against mine. Two or three of them opened their shops very close to me, and they would do a lot to try to ruin my business. I would pay the brokers and growers who sent me fruit as soon as they sent their goods to me, then sell off what they'd sent at the market rate. But this wasn't how these other shops worked. They would wait to sell their goods until I had sold whatever I had. Once I had nothing left, they would sell their fruit at a rate that was ten rupees higher than mine. Then they'd note this rate on the list of goods that they sent to the fruit brokers.

The brokers would come and ask me why I'd sold their fruit for a much lower rate. "Ayya, at what rate are you selling our fruit? I've lost ten rupees on what I gave you."

"I can sell the fruit only at this price. If you want to send your goods to me, send them. If not, you can go somewhere else," I would have to tell them.

"Let them do whatever they want," I eventually decided. I didn't want to quarrel or fight back against any of this, and I decided eventually to let it all go.

I even found some happiness then, as the business began to decline. I had been struggling to manage all the fruit that came to the shop. There was so much that I had to give out on credit each day and then collect back in return. And at the time, I had no one else to help me. I was tired, toiling throughout the year without a single day of rest. "Enough of this working for 365 days each year," I thought to myself.

There was a time when I wanted to earn a lot of money. Then that began to change. I had enough of an income, I was satisfied with what I had, and I lost the desire to keep earning a great deal of money. If I needed something more, I would trade a little more. Otherwise, I kept the business small. "Who needs to bring in so many goods, then suffer when they don't sell?" I asked myself. As the children grew up, I began to feel such things more and more.

To trade in fruit: this was the hand that I was dealt. It was difficult work. I had to be at the shop by five each morning. Each afternoon, I'd have half an hour at home to eat lunch, and then it was ten or eleven at night before I came home again. I'd go to sleep at midnight, and even then, I'd keep on thinking: "This much is due from him . . . That much is owed to someone else . . . How can I get back what I lent there . . . ?" This is all I could think about, twenty-four hours a day. That was how I had to toil.

I was never able to spend time with the children. And so I began to ask myself: "Why should they also grow up to do something like this? Let them work on their own. Why should I keep doing this? Maybe I ought to close up this shop and do something else to help them out."

My oldest son, Ganesan, had already begun his practice as a doctor. "Could I work alongside him, as a drug compounder?" I thought to myself. But nothing like that came to pass. He went off to America, and I kept on trading fruit until the end of my working days.

Senthikumar was my fourth son. He never found a proper job, and he wound up in the shop with me. He had applied for a seat in an agricultural college, which was a good thing: agriculture, after all, keeps us all alive. "Suppose we had an orchard ourselves—then we could produce our own fruit," I imagined.

But Senthi never got a seat in that college. He finally finished an MA in Tamil literature, and though he tried very hard to find a job, nothing came his way. Around the same time, I also had to make a trip to America, and so I brought him into the fruit shop and taught him what I knew.

In 1984, we registered the shop in Senthi's name. "Do as you wish with the business," I told him. Though he took charge of the shop himself, I would also go each day to help him out. Whenever there was a big crowd of buyers, I would work out some of the deals myself. I shared whatever I could of my experience, so that he could run the shop without me. Gradually, I passed all of these responsibilities to Senthi.

Senthi began to look after everything on his own. But because the climate for this kind of trade had also begun to change, there was less and less business each year, and I had more and more time to spend at home. I would go to the shop every now and then—once every ten days, or just once a month. Now, for the last five years, I haven't gone there at all.

Even so, Senthi's business still depends on my name: M. P. M.

∾

# MADURAI FRUIT MERCHANTS ASSOCIATION, 1960

# 17

In India, as elsewhere, the modern city is known as an engine of growth, a vehicle of social and personal transformation. Whether concrete spires or towering plumes of smoke, the city's products are visible even from a distance. More difficult to see are the innumerable things that fuel these developments—an endless stream of resources drawn from hinterlands near and far, prey to omnivorous and often indiscriminate appetites.

It may sometimes seem as though these mechanisms of extraction work with a brisk and automatic momentum of their own. But overseers, agents, and laborers are needed at every stage to turn natural elements like fruit into commodities. And value is always a mystery, when it comes to the commercial markets and bazaars that put such things into circulation. Prices are fixed through transactions fraught with power, danger, and deceit—even when their parties are clad in pure white clothes and amiable smiles. Like these men, for example.

The year is 1960. These twenty-three men represent the fruit sales commission agents of Madurai. Ayya is standing in the second row, between K. Narayana Gounder and S. P. Ramasamy Pillai. Ayya's elder brother, M. P. Gurusamy Nadar, is seated in the first row, and beside him, in white slacks, is N. Kannayiram: owner of the Central Theatre on Mela Gopuram Street and one of the wealthiest and most influential merchants in the city.

Murugesan, Ayya's third child, knows most of these men. He and his brother Gnanam often wander over to their father's shop in the evenings after school. They know where they can find him: at his desk, close to where he keeps his cash box. Sometimes they want a few annas to watch a movie. Sometimes, it's a *dosai* that they are craving.

"What's this that's come?" Ayya asks.

"It's nothing," the boys say.

"What, are you hungry?"

"No."

Ayya might take them to a restaurant, the Jyothi Ananda Bhavan, buying just one *dosai* for the two of them to share. He might have a coffee or a tea there himself, but that is all.

Murugesan has duties of his own at the shop, whenever he's on leave from school. He sweeps the veranda and the road in front of the shop each evening and washes them down with a bucket of water. When he was younger, he used to help count out the fruit. Now, he's begun to write out the list of goods sold on behalf of each fruit grower or broker.

There is a ledger that records how many baskets of fruit were sent by each vendor and the price at which they've sold. Sometimes, the price recorded on the list of goods is the same as what is recorded on the account books. Sometimes, the price recorded is 10 percent lower than the price at which the baskets were sold. This margin, he is taught, is something like insurance.

A vendor might take an advance, then send his fruit to someone else. Then there are those who disappear without paying at all for the fruit that they've been given on credit.

Murugesan writes out each bill of payment onto a sheet of carbon paper. The original has to be sent by post and a cover letter prepared for each of these bills:

> To the Great and Esteemed Mr. Arumugam of Thandikudi—
>
> Greetings from M. P. M. in Madurai. We have received the twenty baskets of oranges that you sent through God's Grace Lorry Service. We have sold those, and include here the bill of payment. We have arranged to send you by money order the 78 rupees owed.
>
> Affectionately yours, M. P. M.

Printed above the handwritten words on each of these cover letters are Ayya's contact details, which include his telegram address, "neembuwala Madurai"—the lime-man of Madurai. They also include the phone number of a nearby business, Habiba Lorry Service, that takes his calls.

Some evenings, Murugesan follows behind Ayya as he goes on his collection rounds. Ayya might buy him some snacks to eat or a drink from a stall beside the Imperial Theatre. The father introduces his son to the other merchants and to the street vendors who buy their fruit to sell once again to the city's residents.

"Who's this?" they ask.

*Enga kodukku,* "my boy," he might say to those whose language is Telugu.

Murugesan is still young, but he is troubled by what he sees on these rounds. Each fruit vendor sells her fruit on a particular street or corner. The merchants are ruthless in extracting their dues from them. The women keep their money in small drawstring pouches, cinched tightly at the waist of their saris. "I've got no money," the women try to say, but the merchants grab the bags from their waists and take whatever they can find there.

At their shops, the merchants pick up their fruit five at a time as they count them out for the women who will sell them: 5, 10, 15, 20, 25 . . . This count, however, always begins not with a number but with a word, *lapam,* or profit. "*Lapam,* 10, 15, 20, 25," they say.

To Murugesan, it looks as though these traders are exploiting the women with whom they work. He empathizes with their plight. A few years later, when he enters engineering college, he will become a staunch Communist. This is before he'll join the Indian Air Force, and well before he'll leave the air force for the global trade in software.

∽

# BRANCHES IN MANY DIRECTIONS

# 18

I CAN REMEMBER HOW I TORMENTED AMMA ONCE FOR A PENCIL, back when I was studying in the second grade in Pudur. It was all because she had refused to buy me one. Pencils came from Japan in those days. They didn't make such things in India, when the British still ruled the country. We each had slates and a black stick to write with, called a *palappam*.

Amma had gone out one day to collect some water. There were no tanks or wells close to the house, and she had to go all the way to the common well to get whatever water we needed for the house. She was going to the well that day, as she did every day, along the same path that I took to school. And as I was walking to school, I saw her on the path ahead.

I ran behind her, grabbed onto her waist, and began to shout, "I want a pencil! I want a pencil! Buy me one before you go!"

I stopped her right there and wouldn't let her go any farther, that's how troublesome I was. I knew she wouldn't listen to me unless I did this. "I won't let go, I won't let go," I kept saying, grabbing onto her sari. The sari was beginning to come loose. Finally, she couldn't stand my mischief anymore. She went to a shop to buy me a pencil, before heading again to the well.

At the time, one pencil cost just half an anna. There was nothing else I wanted so badly then—I had no other desires, just this pencil-desire. In those days, we used knives to sharpen such pencils. I remember how I kept shaving and shaving that pencil with a knife, until there was nothing left at all. By the next day, the whole thing was gone. All out!

When it came to raising our own children, I can't say that I did very much. While they were growing up, I had too much work to do, hardly any time away from the shop. Their mother was the one who raised them, and I hardly paid any attention to what she did. From time to time, when there was something needed from me, I would make sure to do it. Otherwise, their mother took care of whatever problems that came, as problems always do with children. She would take them to the doctor. She would buy all their clothes. I gave them money, that was all.

Chellammal and I fought about just two things: money and God. When it came to the children, we both felt the same way: whether it came to raising them, educating them, or looking after their marriages, we would always agree on what to do. I never tried to do anything against her wishes, nor would she act against my own.

The boys, they would ask for everything. "Buy me these books . . . Pay these school fees . . . I need a bicycle . . . I want to go to the movies . . ." If they wanted something, and it seemed all right to me, I would give them some money. Our daughters, though, never asked for so much: they might want to buy some books, go to the temple, or go out with their mother, that was all.

Even then, girls weren't sent to school once they came of age. This was why our Rupavathi studied only until the eighth grade: once she came of age, we made her stay at home. The poor girl, always at home, what could she have done? For two or three years she didn't go anywhere else. She was bored, and fights often came between the girl and her mother. "Do this, do that," Chellammal would always tell her, and Rupavathi would refuse.

I was worried because this kept happening. We decided to fix a marriage for her, and we began to look for a groom. One day, one of my sisters came crying to me—she was younger than me by three years. "Don't look for a groom anywhere else. You've got to marry her to my son," she insisted. Rupavathi was sixteen years old at the time, and the boy was seventeen. We agreed and held a wedding for the two of them. It must have been 1962, when that wedding took place.

In 1969, Rupavathi died. What happened, how she went, it's all still a mystery to me. Everyone has a different story, and there's no proof, one way or another. I was at the shop when I got the news. I rushed to Chennai, where she had been living. No one expected this to happen.

Our own daughter. How she cried, my wife. Though she'd had eight children, she couldn't bear to lose a single one of them. For seven or eight years, we suffered that loss. Then, as the days passed, we arranged a wedding for Ganesan, and then another wedding for Raji. Slowly, things got a little better once again.

Chellammal and I sometimes talked about what the children ought to be doing, though we never had the time to discuss such things very deeply. They studied well and grew up well, almost by themselves. Ganesan was the oldest of them. Because he did so well in school, all the others began to study like him. If Ganesan hadn't worked so hard and become a doctor, if he'd gone into business or even farming, for example, none of the other children would have studied either. They all learned what to do by watching what he did.

Jawaharlal Nehru was prime minister of India at the time, and there was a lot of talk about national development. I also wanted my own children to do something important with their lives. These were the circumstances in which they grew up.

Ganesan was very good with the shop's accounts. For two years, he came to the shop each day to do the accounts, until he was in the tenth grade at school. Then he came one day and complained to me. "If I keep looking after the accounts, Ayya, my studies will suffer," he said. So I hired someone else to handle this work.

Chellammal's uncle in Pudur, Shanmugavel Nadar, wanted Ganesan to quit school and come back to the village to look after their fields. But Chellammal and I didn't want this to happen. As a trader like me, or as a farmer, he would never have the kind of respect that doctors enjoyed. Everyone thought of medicine as the best work.

It was very difficult, though, for Ganesan to get a seat in a medical college. Admission took recommendations and a lot of money. At first, we didn't consult anyone about trying to get him a seat—we didn't know anyone who could have helped with this, anyway. Then I went to our family doctor and said that we'd put in an application for Ganesan to study medicine. There was no one else I knew with any influence.

"Please try and help us," I told him. "Let's see," he responded. Ganesan didn't get a seat that year, and he joined a bachelor of science program at the American College in Madurai. Finally, the next year, he was admitted to Madurai Medical College.

Ganesan studied there for a bachelor of medicine degree, and then he completed his MD. He scored very highly on the service commission examination, and there was even a chance for him to go abroad. Ganesan hoped that what he had learned would be of some use to his own country. So, rather than open a clinic of his own, what he most wanted was to teach medicine.

He went to America to study further on a fellowship and came back to work in a hospital here in Madurai. Though he had passed the examination for the American Board of Cardiology, no one wanted to hire him as a cardiologist. They even tried to post him to a department of anesthesiology.

Ganesan wanted work that suited what he had studied. We had to find someone to recommend him for a posting, and he was finally hired in the Madras Medical College Department of Cardiology. His seniors there knew very little about all the techniques that Ganesan had learned in America. Despite all that he knew, they still looked down on him.

My son wanted to teach the medical students at the college about some of the things he had learned in America. He planned one lecture for them on a day they were all on leave. "I'm going to teach you what I've learned about cardiology," he told them. They agreed, and he began to prepare slides and other things for his lecture. But when he went to the lecture hall, he found only three or four students sitting there. Everyone else was more keen on cricket, and they had all gone to watch a match. The boy was heartbroken.

"Fine," he said to himself, and gave the lecture to the few students who had come to listen. This was the kind of work he had in India: work that placed no faith in what he'd learned, work that gave him no chance to prove his talents. He opened his own clinic in Madras to practice medicine and kept it for some time. Then he decided suddenly to go back to America, and he left with his family, just like that.

As the children grew up, my wife and I did not want to advise them about their work: "This is what you should do," or "You shouldn't do that." What learning did we have, such that we could give this advice? We toiled, we struggled—that was all we knew. The children studied on their own and pursued their own work as soon as they had finished. This is what we wanted.

Murugesan wanted to study engineering, but it was very difficult to get a place for him in an engineering college. He finally managed to get a seat that was reserved by caste. As Nadars, we didn't belong to a high caste, nor were we among the lowest castes. But there were seats also reserved for those who belonged to middle castes like ours, and he gained admission through this quota.

While he was still in college, Murugesan was selected for the Indian Air Force. They gave him orders to join the air force training program as soon as he'd completed his engineering degree. His mother was worried. "I'm not happy with your joining the air force," she told him. "Flying planes is a dangerous job. This isn't something you need to do." She even stopped him from joining later, after he'd already finished his training.

Rather than just sit at home, Murugesan came to the shop for about a month. But he didn't enjoy the work at all, and he insisted again on rejoining the air force, as he had wanted to do. His mother was anxious about this decision. "I don't like the idea of you going back to the air force," she told him once again. "That's dangerous work. Look, isn't it electrical engineering that you've studied? Can't you at least get a job with the Electricity Board?"

He agreed to try this and put in so many applications for such jobs. But though he tried for three months, he couldn't find a government job. It didn't seem likely that he would find such work at all. Nor were there private companies of that kind in Madurai back then, not as many factories as there are now. Finally, Murugesan went back to the air force once again.

In those days, the air force was a respectable line of work. Murugesan even knew how to shoot a gun, and because he was my son, people were afraid of me too. Once, there was someone collecting funds on behalf of the fruit merchants association, to contribute toward the war with China.[1] He asked me for a donation, and I gave him a small amount. "Ayya, you do so much business, and yet you give so little," he said to me.

"My son's an air force officer," I responded. "There he is, working to protect the country. You want money from me to support the war, but I've given up my own son. I can't give anything more than this, and yet you're asking me for more?" He went off without a word.

While he was in the air force, Murugesan was transferred to many different places. He went all over India. He and his wife had two children, and wherever they went, the children had to study in that language: one language in Gujarat, another language in Patna, Oriya in Orissa, and so on. Mysore, Bangalore, Delhi, Madras . . . As the military kept moving him from place to place, his rank also climbed. He served in the air force for fifteen years, until he'd become a wing commander. Then he decided this was enough and took voluntary retirement.

I was never one to tell the children that they ought to do one thing or another. Their mother, though, was willing to say such things to them. She would tell me all her worries. "Fine," I'd say to her, "you do as you wish."

What I knew was the fruit trade, and nothing else. This was all that I was able to study, these were the lessons of my experience. What the children had learned was something else altogether. Doctors learned how to save lives. Engineering had its own subtleties. There were important differences between these things. I believed that each of them would come forward in life with what they had studied. It wasn't right for me to try to make decisions for them, given what I knew. It was best to leave them free to do as they wished.

As they grow up, children ought to listen to what their parents say. There are things that we sometimes tell them, questions that we have to ask: "Be there on time, don't come late . . . They let you out of school a long time ago, where have you been until now? . . . Who were you playing with? . . . Where did you go?" When we ask such things, they ought to have good answers.

In our household, my wife was the one who asked these questions. I never had the time to look into what the children were doing. But, if they ignored what she said, I would also speak my mind. I wasn't one to try to correct the children by hand—it was always with words. If they listened, they listened. If they didn't, they didn't. By the age of twenty, everyone makes their own decisions for themselves. By that age, responsibility comes automatically, on its own.

We didn't raise our children by ordering them to do this or that. They studied as they wished, lived as they wished. We never searched out work for any of them: they always looked for jobs themselves. And when it came to marriages as well, we never felt that alliances ought to be made only with certain kinds of families and not with others. They would come to us, and these things would also work out on their own.

Gnanam, for some time, was a troublesome child. He studied well, but he had many friends, and he was always wandering around with them. He was very mischievous too, but he would insist that we let him do as he pleased. Then, over time, things got better. He had wanted to study engineering, but Ganesan told him that he ought to study medicine, like him. Ganesan got him an application, filled it out himself, and took Gnanam to Madras for the interview. He got a seat to study at that college, and Gnanam became a doctor.

While he was studying there, he fell in love with a girl from another caste. He was stubborn. "I'm in love with that girl. She's the one I'm going to marry," he insisted. In those days, people were very cautious about intercaste marriages. Parents would never consent.

His mother refused to allow the marriage. Then he somehow found a way of convincing her to agree to the wedding. They didn't talk about this face to face, but he wrote her two or three letters. "If you hold this marriage as I wish," he wrote, "I'll be the first to take care of you as long as you live." Saying this, saying that, he made all kinds of promises to his mother.

"If all of you agree to this wedding, then I will also consent," Chellammal said to all of us. What mattered most was what the children wanted for themselves. That girl, Nallini, was a doctor, and he was also a doctor. They got along well and would have a good life together. Why should we worry about such things?

After the wedding, Gnanam, like Ganesan, went off to America.

Senthi completed an MA in Tamil and joined me in the shop. Raji studied until the eleventh grade, then married one of Ganesan's classmates; they also went and settled in America. Once Meena had finished her bachelor of science degree at Lady Doak College in Madurai, we found her a groom who had studied law and was working in a government office in Madurai. Kannan got an M.Tech. degree at the Indian Institute of Technology in Delhi. Each time he moved from one software company to another, his salary would increase ten times over. All of them were good children. Watching their progress made us happy indeed.

They all settled down in various places: some of them stayed here in Madurai, and others went to Chennai, Bangalore, and America. It was true that their mother and I felt some sadness, as so many of our children went to live in such different places. It felt as though they were leaving us behind, for places very far away, places that we could hardly see. Chellammal was especially upset, but then she would console herself with the thought that they would have good lives wherever they went.

The children too would do their best to comfort us: "Ayya, Amma, we'll always look after you. We'll be abroad for just some time, and then we'll come back to India," they would say, always reassuring us before they left. That sadness would remain with us for some days. And then, we would begin to feel better once again.

Ganesan was living with his wife, Lalitha, in Madras when he first told us that they were going to America. This was hard at first for me to hear, I must admit, but he tried to console me. "You don't have to worry about anything, Ayya. I'll just earn a little money there and come back again soon. It's in India that I plan to work," he said. Then, when he went to America, he assured us once more: "Everything I earn is for you, isn't it, Ayya? Don't worry."

When his children were born there, he promised that he would bring them back. But then as they grew up, they began to study in schools there, and as that culture, that knowledge, became part of their lives, Ganesan and Lalitha began to worry about what would happen to the children if they came back to India. "With the situation in India, they get diarrhea often," they told us. "They're bitten by mosquitoes. India doesn't agree with them."

What could we do? "The grandchildren don't always have to come with us to India, but we'll at least come back often to see you," our children in America began to say.

Isn't this what life is like? Something sad may happen, but that feeling of sorrow always remains for just some time. Slowly, it becomes something else.

"They're leaving us behind to go somewhere very far away . . ." Say this too often to yourself, and you might begin to feel very uneasy indeed. But then they would send you a letter from wherever they went: some happiness. Then they would call you by phone: more happiness. Then they would come back to see you: even more happiness.

This was how we had to satisfy ourselves with their being so far away. After all, they were also seeking progress in their own lives. We were proud, too, that our children had gone as far as America to earn a living. We had done whatever we could to educate them, and now they were all working on their own. We never asked for anything of what they'd earned. Not once did we ask any of them to give us some of that wealth.

You ought to be able to face whatever comes, without depending on anyone else for charity. We never expected much from our children, but they always helped us anyway. What they chose to do for us, on their own, was always helpful. They've done so much already, and still, even now, they do so much for me.

∽

# NORWALK, 1974

# 19

There are more than 20 million people of Indian descent living now beyond the bounds of the Indian subcontinent. In the colonial era, this diaspora followed the tracks of the British Empire. Indentured laborers worked plantations and mines in the Caribbean and South Africa. Traders pursued commerce in Singapore and East Africa. Sikh soldiers who had served in the Indian Army migrated into California, finding work in farms and lumber mills until Asians were barred from immigrating to the United States in 1917.

The relaxation of American immigration laws in 1965 induced a flood of migrants from India and other Asian countries. Many of these Indian immigrants wound up driving taxis or working in hotels and restaurants, but a significant number were skilled professionals, recruited to serve as doctors and engineers. They had been trained at government expense to meet the needs of national development in India, but the lure of America was difficult to resist. Advertisements for prospective grooms in Indian newspapers began to reflect these new horizons of desire, as "green card holder" became a prominent feature.

This was how Ayya and I wound up together in this small, two-bedroom apartment in Connecticut, on the northeastern coast of the United States. My mother and father had just moved here from New York City so that he could begin a hospital fellowship in cardiology. The apartment was fully furnished by the hospital. They needed to buy only a few cardboard boxes, for a dollar each, to carry over their clothes and possessions.

Ayya and Paati had already been in New York City for three months. They came to America for the birth of Raji Athai's daughter, my cousin Vasanthi—her father, also a doctor, had studied with my father at Madurai Medical College.

My mother was expecting my sister at the time, and Ayya and Paati stayed on for her birth too. When Ayya first took her into his arms, he thought of his mother in Pudur. "Here's my Amma, born here," he said, looking down fondly.

At the time, I was less than two years old. I used to follow Ayya everywhere, I am told. He, unlike my mother, was always willing to indulge me. With apple juice, for example. "Ayya, ayya," I'd say, taking him by the hand, walking him to the fridge, pointing out the bottle inside.

For these newcomers to America, Western goods were powerful attractions, symbols of a sophisticated life. This photograph, for example, was taken with my father's new camera. He had framed the picture very carefully, making sure to capture the square table with its lamp, the studio portraits on the table, and most importantly the tape recorder. They were proud of this device, which they had recently bought on Canal Street in New York City. A dual voltage model, it would also work when they went back to India, as they still planned to do.

In the eyes of these visitors from India, desire crossed easily into temptation. Whenever Ayya went to the stores nearby, he would calculate the cost of things in Indian rupees. Everything seemed to teeter on the edge of an unnecessary and even dangerous expense. Just how many tomatoes did they have to buy? Exactly how many onions did they really need? "Just buy this much," he would warn my mother.

Paati also had advice on how to handle the enticements of the American marketplace. "You shouldn't buy everything that the children ask for," she told my mother. "Show them that you can't do anything more than this. They'll understand only if we tell them."

༄

# BETWEEN MADURAI AND AMERICA

# 20

I CAME FROM PUDUR TO MADURAI IN 1947. I'VE LIVED IN THIS CITY ever since. We've rented so many houses here over the years. First, we lived on a small lane near Muni Street. We paid just ten rupees each month for that house. In 1953, we moved to Lakshmipuram and lived there for sixteen years, until Rupavathi died. "We've lost a daughter," her mother kept saying. "Let's clear out and find somewhere else to live."

We lived well in that Lakshmipuram house. The children always played outside, on that small lane. There was some empty space above the house, a roof terrace. I put up a thatched shed for the children to study there and ran an electrical line so that they would have light when they needed it. I bought a big desk to keep on the terrace, big enough for four of them to lay out their books and study at the same time.

Ganesan was always reading up there on the terrace, sleeping there as well. Down below, inside the house, there were three rooms:

six of us would sleep in one room, and two of those rooms we rented out to other boarders. For a long time, this was how we lived in Madurai.

There was a well within the house, where water would slowly seep when it rained. We would drop a bucket by rope to draw that water, but when it didn't rain, the well ran dry. Chellammal would walk to the bank of the Vaigai River for water to bring back home. Dig a hole in the sand on the edge of the river, and water would rise up just like that. That was what we drank at those times. There were even tiny fish in that river that we would sometimes catch—no bigger than an inch and a half in length.

Madurai in those days didn't have many restaurants. "Let's find a place with good coffee to try out," Chellammal would sometimes say. There was a place called the College House Restaurant, which was quite famous for its high-quality "degree coffee." For an extra anna, they would flavor your coffee with some kind of essence that gave it a pleasant flavor.

Then there were the exhibitions on the Tamukkam fairgrounds. You could go there by cycle rickshaw or auto rickshaw, but we would always take the bus. How else could we afford to take eight children? There was a bus stop near the Chintamani Talkies cinema hall, very close to the house. From there, each bus ticket cost one and a half annas. The next stop was at the rice market. It was some distance away, but a bus ticket from there cost just one anna. I would walk everyone from home to the rice market and wait to board the bus from there—just to save those few annas.

The exhibitions would show off new things for sale, things that had just arrived. Each of these things they would introduce to customers, one by one. Most people at the time were still eating and drinking from earthen plates and pots, while in the exhibitions, you could see plates and pots made from stainless steel. "Buy these to use at home, and they'll last throughout your lifetime," the dealers there would promise.

The younger children, meanwhile, would get hungry. We would look around, buy them something to eat, and then go home. We never bought anything for the house at the exhibitions. It was difficult to carry such things when we already had to bring the children home safely. We would look around and remember what we liked. Then we would go and buy the same things in the bazaar, where they were always available for the same price.

It was when we were living in Lakshmipuram that I bought an Echo radio for the house. It was an Indian model, built like a very big box. They never broadcast dramas back then, only the news and songs. Each day, I would listen to those programs for some time. Nowadays on the radio, you hear Tamil, English, and Hindi, all mixed together. But what they spoke on the radio then was only the purest Tamil.

The Chintamani Talkies was very close to that house in Lakshmipuram. Crowds of people would come to that theatre. They always showed Tamil films: mythological stories, or stories about the love between husbands and wives. The same people always sang and acted in the films. I enjoyed the performances of M. S. Subbulakshmi and Thiagaraja Bhagavathar most of all.

Once each month, we went to the cinema. It was always very late by the time I came back from the shop. I would stop at the theatre to buy the tickets, and when I got to the house, Chellammal would already be asleep. I would wake her and then go to the cinema hall to find us a place to sit, while she made sure the children were asleep. Then she would lock the front door of the house and meet me there. We would always buy tickets for three quarters of an anna, or half an anna. For that price, there were benches to sit on.

I don't remember ever taking the children to the cinema. The gate of the Chintamani theatre was very wide, and because there were no toilets in the theatre back then, it was there, near that gate, that the men who came to watch movies would urinate. Murugesan, Gnanam, and Meena would go and stand there, watching movies through the bars of that gate. The place was foul, but how could we go and restrain their desires? For them, it was a spectacle. The children even had a name for this—"gate cinema," they called it.

19/4/74. Writing to you, my dear son Murugesan. Everyone here is well. Please write often with news of how all of you are doing there . . . Here in New York, when the sun beats down, people are overjoyed. It seems that summer will last here for the next three months. There too, I imagine, there must be much more sun now . . . Be well, MPM

In 1974, we went to visit America, the America that I'd never seen before. When we walked onto that plane, I was the only one wearing a *veshti*—everyone else was wearing pants. The other passengers frowned when they saw me. "You'll lose all respect in that *veshti*," Chellammal warned me. "Let it go, who needs it," I said to myself and dressed as I always did.

Once we were on the plane, there was no way to go out for fresh air. You couldn't ask them to give you rice. It was no small thing, the way we suffered through that journey. They gave us some kind of bread that we'd never seen before. They even gave us pork. There was some kind of "sauce" that they brought to pour all over this too. I didn't touch any of it.

Whatever I said was half in Tamil, half in English. If they gave me something, "Thangiyu." If I needed someone to step aside, "Egscuce me." If I wanted something from them, I had to wave my hand. Somehow, I managed to do these things, which were also very difficult for Chellammal too. When we got to the airport in New York, her sari got caught on one of the escalators. From then on, out of fear, she never stepped onto another escalator.

The two of us struggled to push along our luggage cart, and when we came out of the airport, Ganesan and our daughter-in-law Lalitha had come by car to meet us. It was marvelous to step outside and see America for the first time. I'd never seen such tall buildings. You had to pay to cross the bridges in that city, but there was no one to take your cash. There was a machine that you would pay, and then that bar across the road would rise by itself. I'd never seen such machines before.

Raji was also there when we got to Ganesan's home, and she was so happy to see her mother and father that she ran to us in tears.

Back in Madurai, before she and her husband had left, Raji would cry each time a letter arrived from America. That's how afraid she had been of leaving. Now I was also very glad to have come this far, to see my children in such a different place.

As an Indian doctor, Ganesan was well respected in America. Once, when I was asleep, Anand threw my eyeglasses down and broke the frame. Ganesan took me to an eyeglass shop. "Doctor sir, please come in," the shopkeeper said. Ganesan introduced me as his father and asked if he could fix my eyeglasses. "We would ask every- one else to pay two dollars for this repair, but it's enough if you pay just one dollar," the shopkeeper told him. We gave him one dollar to change the frame, and then we came home.

To pass the time, I often went to the shops nearby. There was something wonderful about the stores in that city. There were "su- perstores" where you could get all kinds of things in just one place. All kinds of fruit were available at the supermarket. Go to a clothing store, and you would find many different things to wear. There were two or three pieces of each article of clothing, and you could take whichever one you liked.

None of the customers would ever ask how much something cost. The machines showed the cost of each thing, and the customers would never complain or try to bargain. "Please, sir, can you lower this price on this, it seems a little high . . ."—could you ever ask something like this there? "Get out of here!" they'd say and scold you for being such a rustic brute.

We stayed in America for a hundred days. They showed me all kinds of places in New York. There was a park close to where they lived, and I would often take Anand there. "Park, park," he often said to me. He was just a year old at the time. His mother and Ganesan never took him outside. I was the first to show Anand the light of the sun—though he was still very young, he found this delightful.

Until then, we'd never laid eyes on a grandson or granddaughter. We had to circle the globe and come this far to see a grandchild for the very first time. Imagine how this must have been. I kept thinking about him as we came back once more to the airport and sat down in that plane to leave. "What would Anand be doing now? How would Anand be doing now?" I suddenly remembered something that he had said, and tears came spilling out of my eyes.

30/3/74. Writing to you, my dear son Murugesan. All is well here . . . I trust that Selvi is looking after the house carefully. Before you go to sleep at night, make sure to check whether the gate outside, the front door, and the back door are all locked. Tell Subramanian to write me twice a week about what's happening at the shop. Buy him some aerograms and address them for him . . . Wishing you well, MPM

"Such a prosperous place . . . why wouldn't people want to remain here?" I had such thoughts at times, but I never felt the desire to live in America myself. In 1974, two of our children were there, five of our children were here. But even if they had all gone there, I would have still stayed in Madurai. We couldn't leave behind all that we owned and enjoyed here, just to go there. I was comfortable here. I was earning a lot. I had a house and my brothers, my children, and so many others to spend time with. Someone had to look after the business too. Why move there?

At first, the western parts of what is now Madurai—K. K. Nagar, Anna Nagar, Chokkikulam, and so on—were paddy fields. All these areas are now part of the city. The Housing Board had a scheme in 1962 for those who didn't have houses of their own: the government was selling plots of land here to build on.

Ganesan asked me: "Why buy a small plot? Why not buy a bigger plot of land? There are seven or eight of us, and you need enough room for all of us to stay." I thought about what he said and bought a tenth of an acre of land in Anna Nagar for just 13,000 rupees. I didn't have to borrow this from anyone—I had that much money in hand at the time.

For nearly twenty years, that land just lay there. Then, in 1979, we began to build a house, the first that we had ever built for ourselves. I had no expectations of my own about what it should have, or how it ought to look; everything was based on what my wife had thought out. An engineer who had studied with my son Senthi drew up plans for the house, and when they began to build, Chellammal and Senthi looked after everything. It took two or three years to build that house. In 1983, we moved in.

It is in this house that I have been living all these years, with my son Senthi and my daughter-in-law Nirmala. We do whatever we need to maintain it. But if anything breaks or stops working, I won't just throw it out. I'll see if that thing can be put back together or repaired. I'll try whatever small repairs I can do by myself or hire a repairman to do the work. "This can't be made to work, Ayya," he might tell me. Only then will I throw it away and buy something new.

Even when it comes to very small things, I don't have the heart to throw them out. Take a bent nail. Even that, I won't throw away. I'll try to see if it can be straightened out to use again. If it can't be used once more, I'll sell that bent nail as scrap metal—there are so many people who come down our street, looking to buy scraps of metal. If I threw that nail on the ground, someone might step on it and hurt their foot. They would suffer. This is why I never throw away anything like that. Sell it, and there's a profit for me, no trouble for others.

India is a poor country. America isn't like that—it's a country full of wealthy people. There, they throw everything away. They earn a lot, and if they want to throw something away, they just do. They buy cars, and if they aren't working properly, they just toss them aside. I saw something like this happen in 1974. We were standing on the seashore one day, at a place where cars were heaped up as high as a mountain. They were trying to figure out what to do with all those cars. They tried to see if they could dig a hole in the ground to bury them, but that didn't work. Finally, they just dumped them all in the ocean.

Could you dump them like that here? This is a poor country. People drive their cars as long as they can. They'll repair them ten times over, and if they can't fix them, they'll sell them to someone else. Now, in America too, they're beginning to ask such questions—"Can these things be recycled? Can they be repaired?" There, they're beginning to do a little research about these things, trying to learn more about what we do here.

6/1/76. Writing to you, my loving son Ganesan and daughter-in-law Lalitha. Everyone here is well . . . Yesterday, at the house of Raji's in-laws in Tirumangalam, we watched the home movie that you sent. We were thrilled by the sight of the grandchildren dancing, riding horses, and playing with their toys. Please send us more home movies like this, with someone else who's coming back to India from there . . . Be well, MPM

In those days, there was a fondness, a madness in India for all things American. This madness touched everyone. Even we had it back then. In India, I would always wear *veshtis*. When I went to America, I began to wear pants. I had always had a limited number of clothes here. I owned no more than two shirts as long as I lived in Pudur. In Madurai, I must have had five at the most. But after I went to America, that number grew to fifteen, then twenty. At a certain stage, I must have had thirty shirts. At that time, the very thought of a new shirt would stir my desires. Now I don't feel any eagerness of that kind.

Since 1975, in India, I've only bought *lungies* and vests to wear, nothing else.[1] Everything else comes from America. Shirts come. Slippers come. The children keep buying me underwear even, sending it over here, but I never use any of it. I don't even look at the new shirts that come. I have ten new shirts still stacked in the cabinet, all shirts that they had sent me more than ten years ago. New things keep coming, all headed straight into the wastebasket for all I know, unless I give them to someone else.

For Chellammal, though, such desires were never satisfied. There was so much that she wanted. Wherever she went, she would buy whatever she saw. Even in America, she would buy whatever she saw. Here, there were so many husbands and wives lying on a piece of cloth beside the road, without a place to stay, without anything to eat. "At least we've got a house to rent," I would think to myself in those days, feeling bad for them.

What would she think? "Here we are, living in such a small house . . . Look those people better off than we are, look at the house

they're building . . . Look at that bungalow of theirs, while we live in
this tiny hut . . ." These were the kinds of things that she would say
to me.

Even after having had so many children, she had these desires.
"Look at that sari she's wearing. All you've bought me are these
cotton saris," she would say. These saris, she would keep buying them
wherever she went—new saris, again and again. "I don't have this
kind . . . I don't have anything with this design . . ." she would say
if we went to a shop together. When she died, she had ten silk saris
that she'd never worn before. She must have had a hundred saris
from America, all new. Once she was gone, we gave them away to
almost anyone we met.

"I want to buy a sari," she'd say.

"No," I'd say.

We would often fight like this. It irritated me when she bought
those saris, new one after new one. I would argue with her: "Why are
you buying all these unnecessary things?" Then she would get angry.
"The children buy these things for me. What do you care?"

For each of those saris, she would have to buy cloth to stitch a
matching blouse. Each evening, she'd want to walk down to the tai-
lor shop to have this done. "Give me 100 rupees, give me 50 rupees,"
she would tell me every day, before she went.

I could never tell her that I didn't have the money. "Yes, of
course," she'd say. "All that money you've got, who are you keeping it
for? You may not want any new clothes, fine, but this is what I want
myself," she'd tell me loudly.

Whatever she said, I had to respond, or else she would never let
it go. "Fine," I'd say, and just give her whatever money I had. "May
as well work things out," I would think to myself—otherwise, she
would complain to the children. This is what happened once in
America, in 1982, when we were on our way back home to India. We
were in the car, going to the airport, when she complained about me
to Ganesan and Lalitha: "See how he doesn't let me buy anything?
He's got so much money, but refuses to give enough to buy myself
some flowers even."

As the years went by, she had more and more courage of this kind.

4/8/73. Writing to you, my loving son Ganesan and daughter-in-law Lalitha. We are well. We received your letter and the photos you sent. Happy to see them . . . My body is in good health. But I feel tired, without the strength that I used to have. My weight is 66 kilos (145 lbs). I did a urine test, one and a half hours after my afternoon meal. I don't have diabetes. Although I want to lose weight, I cannot. Please write to me about some medicine to lose weight, or to control what I eat . . . Your loving MP Mariappan

When children go abroad, they bring respect to their mothers and fathers. "So, your children are abroad? You're very lucky people," they say in this town, if your children have gone to other countries, if your children have gone to America. But it was only after I developed various illnesses that I realized how far away my two doctor sons had gone and how difficult it was for them to look after me from that distance.

Even so, both Ganesan and Gnanam still know many doctors here in Madurai. "What can we do? We are here, while Ayya is suffering there. Can you please call him?" they would tell these doctors on the phone. "Ayya, please go to that doctor. I've told him everything. He'll treat you well and make you healthy again," they'd say to me.

My wife and I took five trips to America together. Sometimes, when we were all sitting there together, chatting with other Indian doctors, Chellammal would lightly scold them. "You all studied in India at the government's expense, but then you came here without serving your country," she would tell them. She understood the affairs of the world.

I would never say anything like that, but I also believed, at first, that our children would come back here very soon. After all, their mother and father were still here. But then, as soon as they had children of their own in America, all of them forgot about India.

There was something Gnanam once said to me. "I'll earn some money, Ayya. I'll buy a Japanese car to bring back to India. No one in India has ever seen such marvelous cars. I'll drive that car in India, and everyone will think of me as a very important doctor. I'll get so many cases then, Ayya. I'll be able to earn a lot more money that way."

I felt very happy, hearing that he was planning to come back here. I wrote a letter to Ganesan: "When you come, bring back some instruments with you, so that you and Gnanam can start a hospital together." At the time, I had that hope. But this is not what happened.

Three of our children have settled there in America. Murugesan and Kannan have also gone there many times to work. And now that I've given up doing business at the shop, I've been to America ten times myself. Despite all this, the thought of settling there has never occurred to me.

I have all the comforts that I need here. My daughter-in-law Nirmala makes good food that I can easily eat. To pass the time, there are songs, movies, and news running on the television twenty-four hours a day. I enjoy reading the Tamil newspaper, and friends often stop by the house. I talk to them; we play cards. America has none of these pleasures.

When they were younger and used to come here from America with their parents, the grandchildren would complain: "There's something wrong with the water . . . It's too hot . . . These mosquitoes keep biting . . ." We tried to take care of these things as best we could. After all, it's important to look after those who visit. Did they eat well? Did they sleep well?

We arranged marriages for all eight of our children. Then each of them went off to a different place in search of work. They went to wherever they are now, with their own children. But I'm still here, in the same old place—sixty-five years have passed since I first came to Madurai.

Every morning after I eat, I watch a little television. I enjoy hearing those old songs. As I watch, I sometimes fall asleep, and even then, in my sleep, those old memories come back.

༷

# MADURAI, 1992

# 21

Ayya and Paati, together with their children and grandchildren, landed in the mythical heart of modern life, that sweeping cloud of possibility that we call the middle class. It was in the 1990s that this social presence came into its own in India, when a liberalization of the Indian economy propelled a boom in the circulation of consumer goods and the rise of a population dedicated to having them. No longer did families like this one need to make furtive expeditions to black market bazaars, or wait for such things to trickle through the suitcases of their overseas kin. Branded goods were increasingly seen as the gateway to an India of the future.

But being middle class is not just a matter of things and the money to buy them. Narrative and imagination are also crucial—the stories that people tell about their own progress through a world of material prosperity. Media such as magazines, cinema, and television help to circulate these narratives of aspiration and fulfillment. And there are other, more intimate occasions for taking stock, other venues in which middle-class kin tell themselves stories about their own values and achievements, their toil, thrift, and fitness for progress.

Such was the celebration of Ayya and Paati's fiftieth wedding anniversary in 1992. It was the only time that their entire brood had gathered together at once: all of their children and grandchildren, thirty-two people in all. Their wedding was commemorated one morning at the Murugan temple in Tirupparakundram. Then, back home in Anna Nagar, my grandparents received a framed plaque exalting their many virtues in a chaste and flowery Tamil.

Later that evening came the speeches, in a banquet hall at the Pandiyan Hotel. Nearly everyone in the family, young and old, was cajoled into saying a few words. Each time someone approached the microphone, the videographer would throw the switch on his glaring lights, charging the moment with even more panic and nervous laughter.

"Our house was like a university," my uncle Murugesan declared. They owed their knowledge to Paati, who always kept track of which child had what exam on what day, how well he or she needed to do on that exam, and exactly how that child wound up doing. "If our parents weren't properly educated, properly brought up in life, I don't think we grandchildren would have been so lucky," his young daughter Sridevi added shyly.

A college sophomore at the time, I was also swept into the tide of celebratory confessions. "Today's the first time that I really have a sense of the history, the sacrifice, the growth, the progress that is represented in this family, and why we're all here together, and why we're celebrating," I said, in English, while one of my uncles translated for my grandparents.

A sense of mobility was essential to all of these stories, in which education and employment always figured as ways of moving on, moving up, moving out. The grandchildren who spoke that evening would go on to work in Dallas and Los Angeles, Boston and New York, Singapore and London. But what about their grandparents? Like so many Indian elders of their generation, they were sending their progeny to distant places where they would always remain nothing more than uneasy visitors.

By the time Ayya began to speak, the younger children were restless and hungry. "We and our families have advanced in life to a degree that we never dreamed of," he said proudly, smiling despite the wailing that erupted here and there around the room. He asked everyone to remain loyal to each other. Inebriated voices shouted out, "Yes, Ayya! We'll do this, Ayya!"

Middle classes live for the promise of the future, dedicating themselves to securing this horizon. "It's through our children that God has blessed us," Paati said that night. And then my father announced that the next gathering would be Paati and Ayya's sixtieth wedding anniversary, in 2002. "Let's pray to God that both of them will remain healthy until then," he told everyone. Cheers echoed once more throughout that small hall.

∽

# WHAT COMES WILL COME

# 22

TIME KEEPS PASSING, QUICKLY. I MAY NOT BE AROUND FOR MUCH longer. As I get older, small troubles of various kinds will come. Take them lightly, and they will surely grow into bigger problems. And if this happens, I will have to face what comes.

I'm ninety-four years old. Anything can happen at any time. And if it does, I can't keep crying, "It's come, it's come!" What comes will come. This isn't a matter of fate, as people often say—that's just a superstition. We must experience what comes. That is all.

Back when I was still in Burma, I would sometimes go to Rangoon, to buy goods for the shop. We would go there by train, and then we'd load all those things onto a truck and come back on the same truck. The distance there by train was 95 miles, the distance back by truck, 102 miles. I would climb onto the back of that truck and lie down to sleep on top of all those sacks of goods. Something happened one night like this, in 1939 or 1940.

There I was, sleeping on top of all those sacks. The truck driver was coming back at a very fast speed. Suddenly—*padaar!*—the front tire blew out with a big sound. At the speed that he was going, the driver couldn't control, or stop, or even slow down that truck. If he tried to brake, the truck would have toppled over. What could he do? He had to stop it from moving somehow. As he kept going, he saw that the brakes weren't even working. There was a small bridge on the way, where the road passed over a canal. The driver went and crashed into the side of that bridge. The truck broke through the bridge and fell into the canal.

There was the truck, lying on its side within the canal. Everything in the back was covered with a tarp, and I was trapped between the sacks of goods and the tarp. Because the truck had fallen across the running water of that canal, that water, with nowhere else to go, started to climb against the side of the truck. The tarp was getting wetter and wetter. The water was all around me, but because the tarp was stretched so tightly over the top of the truck, I couldn't find a way out. The water kept climbing higher and higher. I didn't know what to do.

There was a railway station close to where the truck had crashed. The stationmaster was still there, along with others on night duty—their houses were also right next to the station. They heard the sound of the crash, and they all came running from the station and their houses to see what happened: men, women, everyone who was there. They untied that tarp and pulled me out. The driver also escaped.

I must have been about nineteen or twenty years old at the time of that accident. That was a dangerous moment for me, but somehow I escaped. If that truck had turned over just once more when it crashed, all those sacks of goods would have fallen on top of me, and I would have drowned in that water. Because the truck stopped moving, when it fell on its side, I survived.

I have absolutely no belief in God, no devotion of that kind. There are no gods. There is nothing like God. Where is this God? They put up a piece of stone at the temple and worship this stone as though it's a god. The temples keep elephants, which pass from house to house along the road, holding out their trunks to ask for money. With all their devotion, people will give something to those elephants. Give it five rupees, and the elephant will take it. But give just one rupee, and the elephant will throw it away. This is how they've trained those animals. It's fraud, that's all.

All these superstitious habits and customs must change, as far as I'm concerned. People shouldn't go looking for differences of caste, religion, or language. Everyone should be devoted to each other, as people of one faith, one kind. This is what Periyar struggled for.[1] House by house, street by street, he waged a campaign concerning these ideas. They held meetings in many different places. I was never involved with his movement myself—back then, I wasn't that concerned about the superstitions that Periyar had fought against. It's only now that I have these thoughts.

It somehow came to me, this way of thinking for myself. "Look at how they're all praying to God . . . Look at how they're wasting all that money . . . Look at all those things they waste in the name of bathing those deities . . . They pour milk, they pour honey, they have a hundred garlands of flowers, isn't all this waste?"—I somehow began to have such thoughts on my own. Now, when I go on my walk each morning, I look at the foreheads of everyone I pass. All of them have *vibhuti,* holy ash, smeared across their foreheads. This means they believe in God. No matter what I try to say about these things, they won't listen to me.

My wife herself was very devout. She would always repeat those words, *om sakthi om sakthi om sakthi . . .*[2] She kept writing down those words, again and again, praying too much, but I could never stop her. Even when she insisted that I go with her to the temple, I would have to bend to her wishes. "I won't come," I might try to say, but she would still somehow manage to drag me there. So I would go along with her, and as she prayed with so much devotion, I would stand there, resentfully, praying without any care.

Chellammal died in February of 1997. She was a woman who had already had eight children by the age of thirty-two. So much weight to bear, that's why she must have died so soon. I always thought that she would die after me. She was also worried that she might go before her husband. But there they went, carrying her off before my eyes. She was fine, but then in five minutes, they said her life was already gone. Did I think she would die like that?

No longer here now to remember me . . . she died while I'm still alive. And now here I am, remembering her.

It was in this house in Anna Nagar that I lived with her. She never wanted to go anywhere without me. She wouldn't spend even one month alone without me. Ten days—we were never apart for even that long. Whenever I had to go somewhere else on my own, she would insist that I had to come back home within four days.

I would tell her that we had to attend some family event some-where. "You go by yourself, I'm not coming," she would say. Then, when I was almost ready to leave for that wedding, or whatever it was, after I had already made a train reservation and bought myself a ticket, she would finally ask, at last: "Can you see if I can also get a ticket for myself?" It was always on that day that she would want a ticket to come with me, the very day that I had to leave.

We were always together. We went to America five times to-gether. Not one day were we ever apart there, not once.

In 1990, we found out that she had breast cancer. She told me there was some kind of lump in her breast. She showed it to me, and I took her to the doctor. They took photographs, scans, and X-rays to see what this was and concluded it was cancer. They took a biopsy and sent it out for examination, to find out how much cancer there was. It was only when we got those results back that we realized what had happened: they hadn't told us how serious it was. We sent the results to Ganesan and Gnanam, in America. They saw the results and told us to come there immediately. Within a month, we were there.

The surgery took place as soon as we got to America, within two or three days. But too much time had already passed. Because the cancer had already spread, the doctor told us, they would have to operate on her again. And then it came back again, just as they said.

She suffered a lot. They gave her chemotherapy and treated her with radiation. Her blood cell count dropped very low. For each problem that came, they gave her a different kind of injection. They looked after her very well there in America.

"Fine, if it must come back, it will come back, let's wait and see what happens," we told ourselves, and we came back to Madurai. That was a difficult time. She was very worried and she would cry a lot. She tried to tell herself that the surgery had taken care of the problem. What could I say to reassure her? How can one person bear someone else's illness? There's nothing to do but to take what comes.

It came back three or four years later, though we didn't know it at the time. We had gone back to America again in 1994. There, Raji's husband was the one who found out, when he heard how she was coughing. We had gone just to see the two of them, our daughter and her husband. But then, when he heard her cough, he told us to go to Los Angeles right away. They gave her lab tests, medicines, and more treatment, and she was fine again. Still, we knew, when we returned to India once more, that the cancer would come back again.

I also had cancer then. It was prostate cancer, not nearly so dangerous. They said it wouldn't spread very quickly, and we could wait two or three years to treat it. Still, it would have been bad if it spread into my bones. Ganesan, Gnanam, and everyone else felt that I should also have surgery in Los Angeles. When all these doctors said that this had to be done, I also agreed—"Fine, let's do the surgery," I told them.

The operation lasted five and a half hours. I had already taken my blood to the Red Cross, and they had saved it. But then, because there wasn't enough of my own blood, we also had to take some blood from them. For those five and a half hours, they kept giving me blood.

After the surgery, they asked me to stay in a hospital ward for just one day. "Your sons are also doctors," they told me. "You don't need to stay here any longer. They'll look after you very well at home." We stayed in Los Angeles for a month and a half. Ganesan and Lalitha took care of us until we came back to India. And then it was Anand who brought us back.

We returned to India in April 1995. Chellammal died in February 1997. She still seemed well at that time. The treatment had gone well. Our sons were sending her medicines from America, and she was taking them all properly. We would go often to an oncologist for checkups. Whenever he asked us to come, we would go at exactly that time. He would look over everything and tell us that she was fine.

Then she began to feel pain, so much so that she couldn't eat. At first, she would eat just a small amount, and then she couldn't eat anything at all. The cancer had spread to her lungs, but we didn't know this yet. The doctor ordered a scan. "She won't live for very much longer," he told us. "Even so, let's admit her to the hospital to see what we can do."

They kept her there for two days. She was still able to talk to us, although she was in a lot of pain. Her pulse kept dropping, so they transferred her to the emergency ward. Senthi and I were the ones who took her there, in a wheelchair. They said that she needed oxygen and gave her a cylinder, with tubes that they put into her nose. But even as we took her there, that cylinder ran out of oxygen. Only when we got to the emergency ward did they change that cylinder and give her a fresh one.

For an hour, the doctors in that ward tried massaging her heart and doing whatever they could. I was waiting outside. Then they came and asked for Senthi and took him inside. He came back out. "Ayya," he said, "Amma's gone." Only then did I go inside to look.

The last thing she had said to me was this: "Where did you go, all this time? The doctors have been looking for you." I had actually gone to try to find a doctor. I saw one doctor standing there, where I went to look—he was the younger brother of one of Ganesan's medical college classmates. But his secretary wouldn't allow me to speak with him.

"It's me, Ganesa Pandian's father," I tried to say. "My wife is seriously ill." But the secretary wouldn't even let me see him. "There's no time to talk about all that. The doctor is very busy right now," he said and sent me away. All of this took some time, and this was why she had asked me where I went.

"Appa . . ." was the very last thing she said. That was all.

What could we do? What would come had come. There was nothing to do but to try to live with it. I must have cried then; I can't remember. But I didn't yell and scream as I cried. Would she come back, if I cried like that? If people do come back for such wailing, then you can cry like this. But that never happens, does it? If someone said to you, "Just wait, I'll come back in a little bit," if they consoled you like that, as they died, that would be one thing. But no one ever says this when they die. When they go, they go.

Her life must have passed as we were wheeling her to the emergency ward. It was a good thing that she went when she did. If she had remained alive, she would have suffered even more. Even Ganesan knew this. We sent him the scans and the reports. It must have been very hard for him to read those reports.

It was difficult for us to convey the news to the other children. Gnanam, Raji, everyone cried so much. As soon as they learned that she was very ill, Ganesan and Lalitha rushed from America to come here. But they got the news in Singapore, while they were still on their way.

In the years before Chellammal died, we slept in different rooms. When she first got the cancer in her breast, they operated and removed one of her breasts. From then on, we would sleep apart from each other. She would sleep upstairs, and I would sleep downstairs.

Then, a month before she died, she told me that she couldn't climb those stairs. "I'm not going upstairs anymore. I'll sleep downstairs," she said. Until the end, that's where she slept, in the same room beside me.

Once her life had passed, we brought her back home, and we took her to the cremation ground the next afternoon. It all came to an end there, when they cremated her. Ganesan was the one who lit the funeral pyre. There were other rituals that he was expected to perform as her firstborn son: shaving his head, arranging a feast for all of our relatives, and so on, but he refused to do these things.

Nor am I one for rituals and traditions. I told them that none of this was necessary. There's another custom called *koduthuni,* where everyone brings clothes for the family of the deceased. "No one needs any such thing," I said.

I am someone who has escaped with his life many times over. When I was a young boy, I once had to go outside at night to urinate. I must have been nine years old at the time. That path back then was full of stones and brush. There were many trees and cactus on all sides of that path—it was like a forest of some kind.

Those plants were full of thorns. And in those days, there were snakes everywhere. They would even come inside the houses. At times you would see a dead snake lying beside the road, a snake that someone had killed and thrown aside.

When I went out to urinate that night, I thought I saw a big snake that someone had killed and thrown onto a cactus. It looked like a very long snake, maybe four feet in length. I saw it lying there, among the thorns on that cactus, and I thought it must be dead. I went up close to try to touch it, but as soon as I put out my hand, it slithered away. I was terrified, and I came running back home. If I had grabbed it and it had bit me, I would have died right then.

When I go, whenever that is, I want to go laughing. The reason is this. The face always looks strange when life leaves the body. And when I'm gone, others will come to see my body. To them, I should be pleasing to look at, like I am now.

None of my children should come with tears and sorrow. "Fine, Ayya lived well as long as he lived, and he fulfilled all his duties," they ought to think. They ought to enjoy that feeling.

I want to die laughing—this is what I want. When my life passes, my spirit ought to be laughing as it goes. It's this thought that keeps running through my mind these days. My children shouldn't even feel that they ought to come from wherever they are in order to attend to my last rites. "As long as he lived, we looked after him well"—this is how I hope they'll feel.

Dying in America would make for a very expensive burial. And it wouldn't be possible to bring my body back to India, either. This is why I won't be going back to America anymore. From now on, I will remain in India.

∽

# 23

There is so much that my grandmother could have said and done to enrich this book, were she still here. It would have been hers, just as much as Ayya's. Paati's powers of description were extraordinary. Even a simple complaint about medicine could swell into an extravagant picture of tablets slipping down the gullet like grains of rice.

The tartness of Paati's humor cut every unexpected situation down to a manageable size. Once, at an Italian restaurant in Hawaii, she dangled the word "fettuccine" over and over across her tongue, marveling in Tamil at the absurdity of its sound and its dubious appeal. She much preferred the tamarind rice that my mother would box up especially for her.

A sense of numbness was with me still when I wrote a letter to Ayya a few days after her death. That letter is gone, but I have what he wrote back, an aerogram packed with the erratic loops and curves of his Tamil script.

March 3, 1997

To my loving grandson Anand Pandian, this is your Ayya writing. I received your letter.

I'm a little better, now that I've seen the encouraging letter that you wrote about Paati having gone to God. Even now, when I think of Paati, tears come unbidden to my eyes. I cried when my father died. In the 63 years since his time had come, only now do my eyes flood by themselves like this. This too will stop in a few days, I think.

I've lived with Paati for 55 years. When the time to go your own way comes, there is nothing to do but pull away. What is there to do? In the last two years of her life, Paati suffered deeply because of her illness. Still, she remained very fond of all of her children, grandsons, and granddaughters.

As doctors, your father and uncle looked after her very well. Even if she'd lived a little longer, she would have felt a lot of pain and hurt because of her sickness. In her final moments, her life pulled away without Paati suffering too much. Even she didn't know that she would go to God so quickly.

In the last hour of her life, myself, your aunt Meena, Murugesan, and Kanna were there with her. We are praying and placing flowers on her photograph and ashes, thinking of her as with us still at home in Madurai.

I heard that you're coming to India in June. Karthik will come in the month of July. Your uncle Gnanam and his family, and your aunt Raji, uncle Annadurai and Ramesh are also coming in July. We will go to the sea to leave her ashes in the water and pray.

Your aunt Meena, Vignesh, Siva, and everyone else are well. How are you? Don't worry that Paati is no longer with us. Study well. Karthik and Vidhya also spoke with me on the phone. They told me not to worry, and said comforting things.

I've lived in this world now for 77 years. I haven't suffered very much in these days of my life. But I've toiled a lot. What I want is for my children, grandsons, and granddaughters to live by my principles.

Your loving Ayya, MPM

What my grandfather wrote on the death of his wife—something in me wants to leave these words to themselves, as though they say whatever need be said about this time of deepest sorrow. Making an example of them now, as I have been doing with his life throughout this book, seems like an especially lousy thing to do.

But then I read, once again, how he draws this letter to a close. Ayya has already put his own life forward, at this most difficult moment, as an example for others to follow. Out of fairness, then, to this gesture, let me try to tell you what I think it meant.

"What is there to do?" Ayya asks. All of us face entanglements with fate. But they have an especially harsh charge in modern India, where backwardness has long been scorned by observers and critics as the consequence of a passive fatalism.

"Study well," Ayya also says. We live, with him, in a time that leads us to look resolutely ahead to the future. But there are also certain moments that remind us that the promise of this future is destined to fall beyond our reach. How to reconcile the pull of our ambitions with our knowledge of their limited horizons? What is there to do?

Ayya is an avowed atheist and zealous opponent of ritual customs and religious observances. He is inspired, in this, by one of the most ardent social critics that India has produced: E. V. Ramasamy or "Periyar," founder of the Tamil Self-Respect Movement in the early twentieth century. Ayya himself has sons in America, doctors whose medical techniques are designed to wage an unyielding war against any indication of the body's fate. What then do we make of my grandfather's invocation of God, twice in this brief letter?

Perhaps this is a moment of moral weakness. But I am inclined to give Ayya—and all those, in fact, who appeal in such circumstances to gods or fate—more credit than this, even if my grandfather himself was unwilling to do so. I never thought to try to learn anything from Paati, while I still had the chance, about her practices of religious devotion. But I would guess that God, for Ayya, is a name for chance, for the essential volatility of life, which always moves like the seas into which he was hoping to scatter my grandmother's ashes.

Indian moral and spiritual lives often seem otherworldly, committed most deeply to possibilities that lie far beyond the world at hand. But this is not where Ayya looks in this letter, as he confronts the death of his wife and the twilight of his own existence.

Life in the world is precarious and chancy. For my grandfather, though, there is nowhere else to look, nothing better than this. To struggle with hope, even in the absence of an assured return, even in the face of so much failure—such is the impulse for progress that he came to share, along with so many others in the world around him. I think my grandmother shared it too.

༄

# BURMA, ONCE AGAIN

# 24

WHEN I WAS A YOUNG CHILD STILL IN PUDUR, APPA WOULD OFTEN go to Burma, while we stayed behind in that village. I didn't know anything about Burma at the time. I never thought that I would go there myself. All I knew was that village.

I never wanted to go anywhere else. I couldn't imagine a future, what kind of person I wanted to become. "In the future, I'm going to have this kind life for myself . . . I'll do this . . . I'll accomplish that . . ."—I never had dreams of this kind. And even if I did think of such things, who would make them happen for me?

But, though I couldn't imagine a future for myself at all, I know that there was a boldness to the way that I took on the tasks of daily life—at least it seems that way to me now, when I look back upon my childhood.

I would go off to pluck *kodukkapuli* fruit. There were thorns on those trees, but without paying any attention to those thorns, and with nothing at all on my feet, I'd climb up quickly to the top of those trees. There was a well below one of those trees, maybe thirty or forty feet deep. The tree itself was thirty feet tall. It was frightening to look down from up there, that far above the ground.

Once, when I looked up from the top of one of those trees, I saw an airplane pass by. This was while the British still ruled India. "What's this?" I asked myself. "Look at how it flies. It looks like a bird, a vulture. The vulture has wings, and so it flies. Can we also fly like that?"

I remember imagining this, looking up at that plane. I remember thinking about whether we could also fly through the sky like that, with our own bodies.

"We swim in the water, don't we? Could we also fly like that, through the air?" This was something that I imagined, that I thought about, when I was still a child in Pudur.

On a Singapore airplane. Having left on Sunday, 27/1/2002, we arrived in Singapore on Monday, 21/1, at 5:30. From there, we left by Silk Air at 9:15 and reached Rangoon at 11:35 in the afternoon. Lakshmi, Parvathi, and Velayi met us at the airport. We called Arumugam and left the Panorama Hotel, and they took us to their house. There, we ate lunch + dinner, and spoke of many things . . . [1]

During the Second World War, Singapore was one of the first places that the Japanese seized. It was when they reached Burma, in the midst of all those battles, that my brother Mutharasu and I came back to India. We traveled by ship, by boat, and on foot and somehow made it back. There were many terrible things we saw along the way. We even left someone behind, someone who was also from our native place. For a long time, I kept thinking about what we did to him. I still think about it, even now.

"I should go to Burma again," I've often thought to myself. "I need to see everything there once more." I had made a living there. That was where I'd learned how to do business. It was there, at the age of thirteen, that I first began to look after a shop.

People from every country lived in Burma at that time. We spoke with them, learned their languages, and gave them what they needed. Only by conversing with so many kinds of people were we able to do business there. And those desires, to converse with all those people, never left me. I wanted to go back. I still feel that way.

My father's tomb was also there; this was something else that I wanted to see. But though I wanted to go back to Burma for a long time, it became very difficult to get in and out of that country. I lost my chance to do so. And I didn't express this to anyone else—never and nowhere did I say anything about this desire.

I didn't speak of these wishes while I was working in that cloth shop in Pudur. I didn't say anything while I was doing business in Madurai, either. No one, in fact, knew how I felt about going back. Why talk about all this? There wasn't even a way of getting into that country. The military government in Burma didn't allow anyone to come or go.

It was Anand who heard all of this from me—he was the first to ask me about these things. I told him everything. And then in 2002, Ganesan and Anand came to talk to me. The two of them had been to many different countries already. "I want to go to Burma," Anand said. "I want to see Burma. Ayya, take me there and show me Burma." And so Ganesan decided to take both of us there. After sixty years, I was going back to Burma again.

When I was young, you could only go by ship to Burma, and it would take three full days to get there. Now we went by flight, and it took just three hours from Chennai to Singapore, and then two more hours from Singapore to Rangoon. In those days, we suffered. Now we no longer had to suffer like that.

At the airport in Rangoon, our relatives came to meet us, those who had stayed behind in Burma after we left: my uncle Muthiah Nadar's children, Lakshmi, Parvathi, and Velayi, and my aunt Kandammal's grandson, Arumugam. They were all much younger than me, for I had come back to India before they were born. They didn't know what I looked like, and I didn't know what they looked like. Even so, they greeted us fondly.

None of them spoke Tamil, but I still knew how to speak a little Burmese. We could also speak some English with each other.

Lakshmi had been a teacher, now retired. Parvathi was a nurse. Neither of them had ever married. Velayi's husband was a Burmese man; they had two daughters together, who were working in shops in Rangoon, and one son, who was still studying. Muthiah Nadar also had one son, Ekambaram. His wife was Nepalese, and he had a business in Brunei, where he lived with his own family.

I was eager to see them myself. We took some things for them from India, some clothes and some things to eat. Whenever we meet someone, we bring them something. This is a matter of duty, a matter of culture.

We spent one full day at Lakshmi's house. They were very affectionate with me, as we ate together and spoke about many things. At the time, those three sisters lived together in a small apartment in Rangoon. I have no idea how they are now.

Arumugam looked after a roadside *dosai* stall in Rangoon. We ate there the next morning, and then all of us traveled together in an air-conditioned van to Okpo. I remembered the paddy fields that used to lie along both sides of the road from Rangoon to Okpo. Now, everything looked parched and dry.

It was 1 PM by the time we reached that town. I had lived there for nine years, but I couldn't recognize anything, at least at first. Everything had changed. None of the signboards made any sense to me. No one recognized me, and I couldn't recognize anyone else.

There used to be Chettiar bungalows along the main road. Now all those houses were gone; they had all been knocked down after a fire. There used to be an electricity company along the main road while I was there, owned by a Chinese man. Even that was gone now.

We searched for the shop where I had done business and the house where we had lived, but those places had also been destroyed by the fire. It seems that everything had burned down—not one building had been left behind. All the rest houses were gone too: where I'd gone to eat all kinds of things, where I'd gone to sleep for some time, the floors above those resting places, none of this remained. It was sad to see.

I couldn't remember exactly where the shop had been. But I remembered that there was a hand pump to draw water, some fifty to sixty feet beyond the old market. With that in mind, I was finally able to guess where Appa's shop would have been, and even the place where the bazaar shop must have been located. "This was where I used to bring a bucket to get water for the shop," I told everyone, when I saw that hand pump.

We met an old woman who was probably more than eighty years old. "Do you know Perakkiya?" I asked her, in English. Appa's name was Piraiyur Nadar, but everyone there used to call him Perakkiya. The old woman smiled when she heard that name. But I couldn't understand anything she said after that.

Then we began to search for Appa's tomb. There was a Buddhist temple on the edge of the town. We followed a path through the temple and out the back, where we found a railway embankment. We crossed the embankment and climbed down a steep slope to a common graveyard. That was where they used to bury everyone: no one was cremated in Burma back then.

There, below that embankment, among those shrubs, was my father's grave, just as it had been before. I saw the letters that I had written on the day he died: 29.11.33. It was my own handwriting that I could see, and it still looked fresh, as it did when I had first written it. The tomb, clean and white in color, also looked as if it had been built very recently. Imagine seeing, sixty years later, what you'd written once before. It was hard to believe.

We spent a few minutes there. We lit candles and incense sticks, then, placing them on the tomb, we prayed. I reminded myself of my father.

Later, we tried very hard to find details of my birth. Those papers had been kept in the iron safe I left behind in the shop—what I'd given to my friend Ko Chit Pon before we came back to India. Anand, Ganesan, and I did our best to find those things. Anand tried especially hard. We went and spoke to many people, but no one knew anything.

Ko Chit Pon's wife used to run a cloth shop, and we went there to ask as well. They told us that my friend had died and that his descendants had gone to Memyo. We struggled to find out more, wandering around for three hours. But nothing worked out.

There was just one old Burmese man who said that he knew me. He was more than eighty years old. People took us to his house, and we spoke with him for half an hour. I can't remember his name, but he said my name, "Mariappa." He told us that three of my brothers had been born in Burma. This too was a wonder.

As we spoke with that man, I wanted to know, more than anything else, about my own birthplace. He said many things about what I used to do and how I grew up there. Though he said he knew me well, I couldn't place him at all. I just kept listening to what he said.

"Really? Really?" I kept asking in Burmese as he talked. But I could hardly understand what he was saying. I just kept asking what I could about where I was born, where I first went to school, questions like that.

We had eaten that morning in Rangoon but not at all in Okpo. We didn't even think to eat, and it was only when we went to Minhla that we finally ate something. That was where Kasi Nadar used to live, where I kept a shop myself for a few months. He was gone, and so was his wife, but his two sons and his daughter spoke very affectionately with us for two hours. They offered us something to eat at the house of Kasi Nadar's daughter-in-law.

It was 10 PM by the time we reached Rangoon once more. We took everyone back to their own houses and went to our hotel to get some rest.

They changed the name of Prome to Pyay. Rangoon was Yangon; Burma was now Myanmar. But Okpo was the same as it always was. It didn't change at all. In fact, it looked ruined—worse than before, without any development.

When I went back to Burma, I thought it would be as prosperous as it was before. But what we saw wasn't good at all. There were no industries and few opportunities for employment. The Burmese culture hadn't changed, but there were many differences between the Burma that I had seen before and the Burma that we saw now.

People were scared, because the government watched so aggressively over everything. I would guess that there were no thefts, no murders. The government monitored the newspapers and televisions. Those who said or wrote anything about the government were punished harshly. Telephone facilities were very limited, and phone calls very expensive. Cell phones would cost thousands of dollars to buy, we were told. The price of computers was also very high.

The Burmese economy was in terrible shape. Goods were expensive. They used to make unique and beautiful things there from bamboo. Handicrafts and handloomed cloth were still made in Burma, and they practiced agriculture, but this was all they did. People there knew no other trades. There were no factories, either.

People had also changed a lot. There were many differences between the present generation and how people had behaved before. In India, people are much rougher than they used to be. That calm they used to have is gone. But in Burma, it's the opposite.

Everyone there used to be very rough with us. "Who's this foreigner, this *kala?*" they would say. They weren't pleasant to anyone else at the time that we left. But now, there's no such talk of *kalas* at all, and they seem to speak in a friendly manner with everyone. Wherever we went, whomever we saw, they looked at us with wonder. "Someone new," they thought and ran to take a look at us. All of this was surprising to me.

There is no caste in Burma, which I believe is a good thing. This isn't the case in India, though they have tried to change this custom in India for fifty years. The government in India has passed so many laws about caste, but none of these laws seem to agree with common practice. What people actually do is the opposite of these laws. The government in India spends so much trying to encourage mixed-caste marriages. It hasn't helped at all.

But in Burma, everyone you see is a mix of different races. There were many Chinese settled there, and they had all married Tamil women, or Burmese women. Like that, Tamil men had married

Burmese women, while Burmese men had married Tamil women.
All this has become very common. In the Burmese language, they
call this *kapya,* which means "mixture." Character, lineage, all these
things have been lost in Burma to *kapya* races.

The day after we went to Okpo, we saw the Shwedagon Pagoda in
Rangoon. This is a Buddhist temple with a tower made of gold: *shwe*
is "gold" in Burmese. I had seen this temple once before, when I was
young. I remember I had found it beautiful at the time—I had never
seen a place like that before. Now they looked just as they had before,
the golden statues of the Buddha and that golden tower. We hired a
guide to show us around the temple, and he explained everything to
us. That night, all of us ate at a Chinese restaurant in Rangoon.

The next morning, we left for the airport and arrived by plane in
Pagan by 7 AM. There were thousands of Buddhist temples there,
and we visited many of them. Many of these temples were very large,
with beautiful statues of the Buddha. There were even temples there
with Tamil and Sanskrit names. We enjoyed watching the river run
along the edge of one temple. In the evening, we climbed to the top
of a tower to admire the beauty of Pagan's temples at sunset.

There were many Japanese, German, and Australian tourists who
were also there with us. But in this Pagan of 2,400 temples, there
was not a single place for people to live. They had all been chased
away by the government, and they were living in poverty across the
river.

We visited roadside shops in Pagan, where we bought some things:
toys, plates, and other items made from bamboo. Anand and Ganesan didn't know the language, and the shopkeeper gave them higher
prices. But I was able to bargain still in Burmese.

*Pai ya ko si,* the vendor would say—this means "198" in Burmese.

"Give it to me for 150," I would ask, and he would agree to the
sale.

The next day, we went back to Rangoon and once again to Lakshmi's house. We talked about the history of the family, and I showed
them the photographs that we had brought from India. I explained

who everyone was, and they looked fondly at all of the pictures. Lakshmi gave expensive gifts to all three of us, Ganesan, Anand, and I.

The next day, we left. Rangoon to Singapore, Singapore to Chennai.

I've kept all the photos that we took in Burma, right here in the cabinet near the telephone. Every now and then, I show them to people who visit the house. I still have a small notebook where I kept accounts for our business there over sixty years ago. And in my wardrobe, I also have the identity card that they gave me for returning from Burma as a refugee.

Sometimes those memories come back to me: how I did business there, to whom I lent money, what I used to say, and so on. At times, those thoughts even appear in my dreams: the shop, the bazaar, those conversations . . . These were the things that I did there every day, before my life became something else, as it always does for all of us.

These memories also appear at times in the train of my thoughts. I remember one friend who had a butcher's shop in Burma. Once each week, he would put out meat for sale. On those days, he would always come to our house to give us some meat for free.

A woman named Karupayi Amma used to work for him, someone who'd been beaten at home and had fled her village. She didn't have a husband, and this man, who had left his wife at home in India, took up with her. Each week, he would bring us meat. And each of those weeks, she would make us a meat curry.

I still remember the faces of one or two people who used to buy goods from our shop. There was a Muslim man, for example, who had a cloth shop in Okpo. He was originally from Ilaiyangudi, and he must have been about ten years older than me. We were very close. Sometimes, when I had nothing else to do, I would go over to his shop to talk. He was a good man, and we used to exchange money at times, when we needed it—he would take ten or fifty from me, or I would take ten or fifty from him.

When the Second World War came, I came back to India without collecting on any of the loans that I'd given out there. They were mostly Burmese, and honest people. If I had asked them back then, they would have paid back what they had borrowed. If they had come to India and saw me here, they would have paid back those loans then. But they haven't found me yet, and I haven't found them. I doubt they're alive anymore.

I am satisfied that I managed to go back once to Burma. But if we had stayed another two days, we could have learned more about the country now. And I can't go there again: my body isn't strong enough to handle the journey, I can't walk very well, and I have trouble eating. I'm very old now.

Still, though, I want to go back to Burma. Even now, I have this desire. After all, I lived there for nine years, and that desire was not fulfilled when we went back. We couldn't find that iron safe where I had kept the details of my birth. And there were the people of that town, I used to eat with them for so many years. We used to wander, stroll around together.

All those hopes keep coming back to me, even now, still.

$\backsim$

# 25

Ayya has been tense today, his voice erupting in frustration as we follow him through the town of Okpo. He can't remember very much Burmese and needs our relatives here to query, translate, and explain. There was the fire that swept through the whole town in 1986. There are the many new buildings that came up afterward. And memory itself is an unreliable guide.

"This is where I must have been born," he says at one point along the main road, looking toward one set of awnings. But this too proves impossible to verify. "I can't find anything," he admits.

Then we approach his father's tomb, following a line of railway tracks beyond the town and down into the shrubs and brush below the embankment. The cement structure looks solid and implacable in the midst of this green tangle, the parallel lines of its design barely deflected nearly seven decades later by the few pieces that have chipped away. Ayya's face breaks into a warm and rich smile when he steps close to the tomb. "It's my writing," he says proudly, pulling out his eyeglasses to look more closely. "Yes, it's my handwriting."

Taking a bundle of pink roses from his nephew Arumugam's hands, he places the flowers at the crown of the tomb. Everyone takes turns lighting a few sticks of incense, one by one, to rest against the tomb. "I can't describe it," my father says. "This is the only contact I've had with my grandfather." Then, with his hands clasped in prayer, Ayya has something to say:

> There's something wondrous about what has happened here. Coming all this way, from one country to another, laying eyes on what I wrote myself seventy years ago, gazing upon this—no one else could have done something like this. But I was able to do it. Nowhere else could something like this have happened.

> The tomb lies beside a canal, surrounded by thickets of thorny shrubs. It will remain protected this way, just like this, for another hundred years. My descendants, their descendants, all of them can come whenever they want, to pay respects to their grandfather, their great-grandfather. They can gaze upon this tomb, just like us. There is a way to do this now, and we can afford it.

Back in the town, he guesses from the blackened trunk of a tree and the presence of a water pump where his shop would have been. We even meet an elderly Burmese man who claims to know him and his father, speaking a few excited words of Hindi. Despite all of this, Ayya remains unconvinced regarding the mystery of his birth.

"We don't know anything for sure," Ayya says, looking into the lens of the video camera that I'm holding. "This is something essential about my nature: only if you prove something directly to me will I admit that it's true."

Indeed, I know this about him. But throughout this trip, there is another kind of truth that Ayya has also been confronting. The journey seems to have inspired, in my grandfather, the opening of an anthropological eye: again and again, what captures his imagination are the differences between two peoples, the Indians and the Burmese.

As his inventory of these differences grows, I begin to wonder how the history of his own displacement has shaped his ecumenical outlook. Ayya was always an outsider in the towns and villages of his life. And now, with his catalog of comparisons between India and Burma, he seems less interested in boundaries to build than in resources for transformation.

Here is where my anthropological imagination meets his. I have to believe that there are many others like him, scattered here and there in contemporary India and beyond, others with this commitment to the possibility for change that history folds into life.

～

# GIVING AND TAKING

# 26

I WAS BORN IN SOME SMALL VILLAGE, SOMEWHERE. I WENT TO
Burma, never thinking that I'd come back to India. If the Second
World War hadn't happened, I would have remained in Burma. I
would have lived as a Burmese man with other Burmese people.
Who knows, I might have even married a Burmese woman.

There was no one to teach me discipline in those days. Amma left
us when I was a small boy. I was still young when Appa died. My
brothers never told me firmly that I had to do one thing and not another. There was no one around to say such things to me. And even if
they had been there, I would never have listened.

I grew up as I wished, lived as I wished, and made it to this place
in life on my own. It was only until the eighth grade that I studied,
before going off to work at the age of thirteen. My schooling was
poor. I know three or four languages. But how many languages
are there in the world? A thousand? Eight thousand? Maybe eight
thousand, eight hundred and eighty-eight, shouldn't there be at least
this many?

All I have are the lessons of experience. With experience, everything may be understood. When I went to Burma, it was only through experience that I learned all that I came to know there: all those tasks, stocking those goods, collecting that money, all grasped through the lessons of my experience. It is through experience that I've gained whatever principles that I've needed in life. I'm studying still, through my experience, and there is so much yet to study.

I was born somewhere, somehow. I've lived in so many ways. But look now at how I am. At first I suffered so much that I sometimes didn't even have enough to eat. Later, my wife and I had good children and we did our best to educate them. Did I ever think that they would all be married like this, with these children of their own, with work like medicine, with good reputations, living as far from here as America? Now I too am comfortable and satisfied. Those who notice are astonished. No one else could have had this kind of life.

Everyone that I spend time with knows Mariappan's story: how he was when he grew up, how he is now, all the places that he's had to run to, how many children he has now, all the places that they've run to, how well they live now, how happy they are, how happy he is, and the peace that he now feels, without a single thing to worry about. Everyone who converses with me knows these things. Ask them, and they'll tell you about me. But no one else knows.

I'm just an ordinary man. My children know me, and the friends I made through the business know me. The other traders who bought my goods also know me. Those who sent me goods also know me—they know something about my principles, my character. But does anyone else know anything about what I've said here?

There are so many ways to think about life. There must be a thousand things to compare life to. In business, we give and we take. We use *kodukkal-vaangal*, "giving-and-taking," to talk about each person's gains and debts. Gains come when others give you money. Debts, *patru*, are what we have to repay to others.[1] I lend to those I trust. If they trust me, they will lend to me. When I lend to them, and they do business with that money, they will gain something from all the goods they have in hand. And when I sell to them, I also gain something.

When someone trades with me, he becomes my customer. He comes to me for whatever he needs, and we develop a relationship. There is affection in such relationships. Many of the people I traded with were close to me. They would invite me to their family events, and I would go because of the fondness I felt for them. These are the relationships that make us human. What good would someone be without any such relationships, if he pulled himself apart from everyone else? Nothing, that's what he'd be good for.

Giving and taking happens even within a family. A son asks for money, and you have to give him something. "Give me a hundred rupees," he might tell you, then save forty for himself and only give fifty or sixty back to you. "Fine," you'll say and take back what he offers. Or, take giving a daughter away. When parents give you their daughter in marriage, you develop a relationship with them, affection for them. And when they make this alliance with you, they also feel that affection. In spite of all these things, is there nothing else but giving and taking in life? Life can't just be measured by rupees—1,500 rupees, 2,000 rupees, like that.

I used to feel the desire for money. At first, there were so many ways that I would try to earn money. I had to lie a little, in those days, when I did business. But it was only through those tricks that I managed to raise eight children, feed them, educate them, and marry them off. Now, I don't feel that desire to earn any more. All the children are well settled, and there's only a little that I need to meet my expenses. Now, I'm just a broken-down old man with no work to do. I need some place to stay and a little to eat, that's all.

I've done whatever was needed for my children. They've also looked very carefully after me. They're still looking after me. Six years ago, I got mouth cancer. It was very difficult to eat, and it would have been even more painful without surgery. The chairman of the Meenakshi Mission Hospital, Dr. Sethuraman, had gone to medical college with Ganesan. As soon as Ganesan explained the matter to him, he called me directly by phone.

"Ayya, I need to talk to you," he said.

"What's the matter?" I asked.

"Your son Ganesan explained your problem to me," he said, and he told me to come to his office right away. As soon as he saw me, he asked me to open my mouth. "I'll give you the number of another doctor, Dr. Amarnath. Please go see him," he said, and called that doctor on the phone right then. "Ayya, Mr. Mariappan, is coming to see you; please check his mouth and do whatever is necessary. Please give him VIP treatment."

They took me there and looked after everything. I had thirty-one days of radiation. For the first ten days, I felt nothing, but then my whole mouth was filled with wounds and sores. The skin on my face became black. They said that blackness would never change, but they gave me an ointment to treat it and all the other medicines I needed. Dr. Amarnath looked after me well.

I had trouble eating for many days after that. But that doctor gave advice about this too: what to eat, where to go to find such things, and so on. He told me what brands were available in America, because my children were there, and suggested that I tell them what I needed to eat. Ganesan and Gnanam brought all those foods for me from there, just as he'd suggested, and this was what I ate until those sores healed.

There were sores on my tongue, my nose, even my ears. My daughter-in-law Nirmala was very careful to apply the different ointments for each of these sores, just as the doctor had said to do. Now, I've gotten used to eating without dentures, without teeth. Nirmala gives me rice and vegetables that are cooked until they are very soft, without too much oil, and with just a little salt and flavor. She's the reason that I've lived until the age of ninety-four. It's Nirmala who keeps me alive, day after day.

My children all look after me. I live out my days in this house with Senthi and Nirmala. My daughter Meena is also in Madurai. Her house is eight kilometers away from ours, and she comes to see me at least once each week. Ganesan and Gnanam call me on the phone once or twice each week. From there, and from Chennai, everyone comes to see me often. The children look after their father very carefully. That's how devoted they are.

Each morning, I wake up at 6 AM. Right away, I drink three glasses of water. For half an hour, I read the newspaper, and then I walk outside for an hour. I used to go to the park to walk, and I'm also a member of the Walkers Club there. But it's very dusty now, because of all the auto rickshaws, cars, and trucks, and so I look for places in Anna Nagar where there's no traffic on the road. I always walk by myself. There's no one else my age on the road.

When I come back, Nirmala has my breakfast ready. With no teeth, I have to eat oats soaked in milk each morning. Sometimes, when I'm sitting at that table, I think of my wife. "Let me just go and see her at the hospital and come back," I might say. Nirmala laughs when I say this. It's just something that I imagine doing sometimes. Such things happen even in my dreams. Our thoughts always drift along like this.

Anand says that the day after his wedding, at a hotel in Kerala, I asked him when he was going to write my history. I could have asked him that, I don't remember exactly. I forget so many things these days. No matter what, it would have been just a stray thought at that time—this is what our thoughts always do, they stray. But Anand, he has fulfilled that stray thought of mine, that drifting thought of Mariappan's.

Mariappan . . . Born to some poor soul, he wandered around all over the place, and now here he is, sitting on this soil, talking to his grandson.

Anand has come to hear what I have to say, and I've told him everything that lies within my heart. As long as I'm around, I'll share my advice with my children, my grandchildren, and my great-grand-children. I will give them my opinions as long as I can. And then, after that, my story will remain as a historical tale. For another five or six generations, people may read it, and they may come to know that someone like me once lived.

I've never liked boasting about myself. I don't like the way that people here are honored in public. And I'm not one to seek out pub-licity. But, if they think of me later, maybe they'll remember me this way: "In general, he was a man who toiled, a man who lived well. He made sure that his children were educated. He was a principled man who was never involved in fights or violence. If you sent him your goods, he would sell them well, and he'd give you what he owed right away. Everyone came to him because they believed that he would treat them honestly. They say that he's a good man."

This is all I want.

I . . .

I'm no Mahatma, no great man. Just a kinsman of the poor, someone who feels for them. Whenever some poor person comes knocking at the door, I try to give what help I can. I've learned the difference between those who are truly poor and those who put on a mask, cheat people, and stock up money by acting as though they're poor.

Everyone's an actor in this country. Forget them all. Try to live properly, with discipline and with care. This is how I've been living all these years.

Tell me—is all of this true, or not?

∽

# LISTENING TO MY GRANDFATHER

27

Some time ago, I had a dream about my grandfather. What happened was very simple. In the dream, I'm in Madurai again. I'm telling some people that I have just a little more work to do. Ayya is also listening. "I need to go to just two more villages," I say. And then Ayya says, excitedly, "I've also been to those places!"

In the dream, he tells me a story about those villages, a story that I can't remember now. He also says that he's already spoken with the same people I'm hoping to meet there.

I remember waking from this dream, in Baltimore, with a feeling of fullness. It seemed that his life and mine had somehow come together in a larger circle of experience.

The dream came at a time when I was deeply immersed in the events of Ayya's life. Expressed there, no doubt, was the hope that he approved of what I was doing with his stories. There was also the sense of following a path that he had already traced, of somehow inheriting his way through the world. In the dream, I was proposing to go places that my grandfather had literally already been himself. So once again there was the idea that he might be pleased with this devotion to his legacy: a proper heir, the eldest son of his eldest son.

All of this was there in what I saw. But there is something else that also strikes me now, something that has a great deal to do with why it has stayed with me since then. Whatever happiness I felt in the dream, whatever excitement that Ayya seemed to express in the dream, these sensations grew from an utterly accidental convergence between our lives.

I was talking, and Ayya happened to be listening. I mentioned some places that I needed to go, and Ayya happened to have been there already. I needed to talk to some people there, and it so happened that Ayya had already met them himself. Somehow, despite the vast difference between the circumstances of his life and mine, we had found by chance the same path to follow. That morning, in other words, I think that I was dreaming about this book that we have written together and the entirely unforeseen way in which it suddenly became real.

This book has grown like the weedy scrub on the outskirts of villages like Pudur: appearing from unlikely margins, sending up unexpected shoots, taking advantage of whatever resources lie at hand. In one way, this book appeared all at once over the course of just a few months, in the way that green growth suddenly colors a rural landscape after a good bout of rain. But in another way, this is a book that has been seventeen years in the making, slowly laying its roots below the surface of his life and mine, preparing for the right moment to break into the light, to mark out a trail for us to follow.

For these last seventeen years, I've been coming again and again to Tamil Nadu, spending many years in villages like the ones I had pictured in that dream. Wandering through the countryside with farmers, shepherds, and laborers, I've pursued a career in anthropology very different from the sober path of improvement pursued by most others in the family.

There have been many times that my aunts and uncles in Madurai, Chennai, and Bangalore have joked, with both surprise and worry, that I might be going mad in all this wandering. But Ayya has been staunchly faithful in the face of all such doubts, believing that there was something relevant and meaningful in these travels.

I never imagined that I would write a book about my grandfather, let alone with him. Looking back, though, I can see how I've shadowed his story so often in the many other stories that I've tried to put into words. I think that my imagination was captured long back by the simple wonder of what we took for granted as the ordinary backdrop of our prosperous urban lives. What could I have been, if anything at all, had Ayya's life taken some other turn?

As an eleventh-grade student in a Los Angeles high school, I wrote a painfully earnest essay about my first visit to Pudur and the small mud-walled house where my father was born. I spent one semester of college on a hacienda in the agricultural highlands of Costa Rica and a year after college volunteering for a rural development NGO in the palmyra tracts of Tirunelveli. Then there was graduate school in anthropology, and many more years spent in villages west of Madurai, trying to make sense of how people here imagined a good life and how they lived with the difficulty of realizing such a life for themselves and for their children.

As an anthropologist, I've been taught to seek out patterns and generalities, things held and felt in common within the vast fold of human experience. But I've also learned that there are always surprises, wonders, and even miracles buried below the surface of the most ordinary places and events. The challenge lies in making these things available for reflection.

Stories help with this, as do the memories that they grow from. Ayya and I have been doing a lot of digging, especially in the last couple of years, seeking to uncover such forgotten remains from buried times. In trying to make sense of what we've found, I've also had to look more closely beneath my own feet, back to the soil in which they too were planted.

All of us who trailed after Ayya were nursed on dreams and reveries of progress and development, eager fantasies of infinite scope. Soon after I first appeared in a New York City hospital maternity ward, high up in the Bronx, my grandparents mailed from Madurai an audiocassette of blessings and lullabies. There was Paati's hauntingly raspy voice—

> For you to bathe he dug a well,
> my darling—your father,
> did he build a temple for you to pray?
>
> He built a mansion for you to study,
> my darling—was it the
> Pandian kings who fathered you?

The brown of my skin disappointed my grandparents—despite my birth in America, I hadn't bested the light complexion that Ayya brought back from his Burmese days. Still, they took heart in the smallest signs of wits and strength: how quickly I'd first lifted my head, how fondly I'd recognized their snapshot images, how keenly I pined already for the straw of my father's Coca-Cola.

They imagined me lording the circumstances of my birth over other schoolboys back in India: "Hey, watch out! Don't mess with someone born in America!" Before I cleared the age of five, they'd already addressed dispatches from Madurai to one Dr. Anand Sankar Pandian.

Years later, a bit of the history driving these hopes came into clearer focus. Every now and then, when enough of the children and grandchildren in India and America had gathered together in one place, a small hall in a hotel was booked. A videographer was hired, a microphone mounted to a stand. And then, one by one, came the speeches: each of the siblings in birth order, followed by their spouses in sequence of seniority, then the grandchildren by diminishing age and stage, all rehearsing their debts to Paati and Ayya.

Painfully awkward, invariably closing with tears, these monologues were lightened only by the booze that two of my uncles kept stashed in a corner of the room. Time after time, the lessons remained the same: however we had grown, wherever we had gone, whatever we had become, all these developments led back to the two of them, to Paati's close attentions and Ayya's ceaseless toils.

The truth of this story was etched with startling clarity, most especially, on the bodies of the men and boys gathered in those rooms. Look at the family photographs. There's an old one of Ayya flanked by his brothers, five men of nearly equal height, their serene glances and neatly pressed shirts emanating satisfaction with sixty-three inches. Then there are all those pictures of my father and his four brothers, each tipping up on toes or pulling the others down to outmatch his siblings, all to little avail as none of them topped 5'8".

Then there are the younger ones, my brother and our cousins, most of whom have reached the six-foot threshold, reared on broiler chicken and sirloin steak rather than on the soured rice flavored with a lone chili that my grandparents enjoyed in the first years of their marriage. One of the smallest among them, I have hardly anything at all on my father, but the pediatrician speculates that my son might one day clear six feet.

Musing on the varied attainments of his children, Ayya invariably begins with one observation: they studied well. Several of them attended American College in Madurai, founded by missionaries from the American Madura Mission in 1881. All of them came of age in the postwar era, when households throughout India were galvanized by Prime Minister Jawaharlal Nehru's visions of planned development and national advancement.

There were tussles at the dining table over who got to eat the mangoes with their curd rice, but also more serious domestic campaigns underway, such as the household newsletter that my father circulated in the early 1960s extolling the hygienic virtues of regular soaping. Many of these children grew into staunch rationalists like their father, ready to decry belief in God or superstition. Ayya's letters from those years are packed with references to entrance examinations, savings schemes, insurance plans, and other vehicles for rational improvement.

Their household was swept into a confluence of several streams of change, surging from many different directions at once, toward the shared promise of a better future. One of these had to do with the caste to which they nominally belonged. By law and custom, they were Nadars, one among thousands of India's "Other Backward Classes." Although caste is often imagined to have endured unchangingly in India for hundreds or thousands of years, this collective label, Nadar, was an identity that did not exist until the early twentieth century. The first government census enumerating "Nadars" by caste was conducted by the colonial Madras Presidency in 1921, two years after my grandfather's birth.

All of this is detailed in a book published in 1969 by an American political scientist, Robert L. Hardgrave. A hardbound copy of *The Nadars of Tamilnad* sits on a shelf in my office at Johns Hopkins University, purchased a few years ago from a bookstore in Berkeley, California. But the first time I encountered this book was in the Madurai headquarters of the Nadar Mahajana Sangam—the Association of All Nadar People—in 1995, shortly after I had graduated from college.

Ayya had brought me here and explained to those in the office that his American grandson had an interest in the history of the community. They pulled out a well-used copy of Hardgrave's book, published in Tamil translation with Nadar sponsorship from the coastal Tamil city of Tuticorin. This is how the book begins:

> Among the communities of South India, the Nadars have perhaps most clearly evidenced the effects of change in the past 150 years. Considered by the high caste Hindus in the early nineteenth century to be among the most defiling and degraded of all castes, the Nadars, as toddy-tappers, climbers of the palmyra palm, suffered severe social disabilities and were one of the most economically depressed communities in the Tamil country. In their response to the social and economic changes of the last century the Nadars have today become one of the most economically and politically successful communities in the South. From among their numbers have come leading merchants, physicians, and educators; in politics, Kamaraj, their most illustrious son, has brought fame to the caste as chief minister of Madras and as president of the All-India Congress Party.

You can imagine why the book might have appealed to the people it described so generously. Hardgrave details the ancestral preoccupation of the Shanars—as they were once known—with the juice of the palmyra palm (*Borassus flabellifer*), a thick translucent liquid tapped from the stalks of the hardy tree and boiled down into country sugar or fermented into toddy liquor. He chronicles their nineteenth-century migration from the palmyra forests on the southwestern coast of Tamil Nadu into the new market towns of the dry interior tracts.

Responding favorably to the attentions of Protestant missionaries, rising leaders from the community organized collective associations, repudiated their connection with the distasteful palm, promoted the development of community schools and mercantile societies, and orchestrated an exhaustive renaming of the caste itself. The Nadar Mahajana Sangam had been so successful at spearheading this collective transformation that by the later decades of the twentieth century, hardly anyone could recall that these decent Nadars had once been derided as Shanar rascals.

A few weeks after I'd first laid eyes on Hardgrave's book, there was another large family gathering, this time at an opulent hotel in Bangalore. For fifty-five rupees each, the coffee shop in the hotel lobby sold chilled glasses of coconut water, from the fruit of another palm species. "Are you proud to be a Nadar?" one of my uncles asked me. He was an engineer by training and had lived all over India.

I found the question dizzying, given where we were and what I'd been reading. But he didn't wait long before scowling at the simple thought of it. "I'm not," he said. "They are crude, unrefined people, and they only evaluate others by how much money they have." And, he added, "they think too much about eating."

The more time I spent with Ayya, the more I learned about the difficulty of such disavowals. Ayya speaks of walking thirstily through the scrub thickets beyond his village as a child, cupping his palms for water from those unwilling to let his lips or hands touch their pots. He tells of learning at a Nadar community school the arithmetic that would propel his advance, but also of being forced out of the school as an outcaste, by the same association that had founded it.

Ayya speaks of following Nadar mercantile and social networks into Rangoon, lowland Burma, and Madurai, and later relying upon the same networks to secure respectable degrees and favorable marital alliances for his children. The first of these children was named Ganesapandian, after an elephant-headed god of the Sanskrit Hindu pantheon and the medieval dynasty of kings that had made Madurai their capital. But it was a small tutelary shrine to Ayyanar in the palmyra tracts of the distant south to which the family would return, time and again, for many of its most significant milestones.

Such complexities remind us that social realities like caste continue to shape collective desires and possibilities in contemporary India. It is too easy to imagine such things as relics of a distant past. Consider, for example, the fate of Nadar toddy-tappers, some of whom still climb the palmyra palm for a living in various rural tracts of Tamil Nadu, limbs scarred and twisted from a lifetime of scaling sixty-foot trunks with bare arms and feet.

I stumbled across a poignant reminder of this when Ayya and I were going through some of his old papers and notebooks one afternoon in Madurai. We found a diary that my father had kept in the late 1960s, when he had begun to see patients as a newly trained doctor in Madurai. One of the first case histories in this diary was that of one Chelliah, thirty-two years old, married with three children. The man was well built and muscular, my father reported, but still struggled to carry out his trade:

> This patient was going about with his work normally. Two years ago he started developing exertional chest pain and giddiness on and off gradually . . . He feels giddy and vomits at times, more so after unusual exertions. Breathlessness on severe exertions is present for the last two years, and is progressive.

On one corner of the page, the patient is identified as a toddy-tapper from the coastal area of Mandapam. But in the neutral language of my father's account, there's no sense of any special bond or kinship between the doctor and this patient, nor any trace of anxiety on the part of the young Nadar physician: no discernible feeling, that is, that he could have been suffering from the same painful exertions himself, had history worked out differently for his family.

May 1998. Ayya and I spend a few days together in northern California. We drive one morning to Muir Woods, a small parcel of evergreen forest north of San Francisco, across the Golden Gate Bridge. The place has the feeling of an outdoor temple, asking reverence for the few original coast redwood trees that remain after the conquest of the American West, some of them reaching more than 300 feet from the ground. There at Cathedral Grove, a circular stand of redwoods, the death of Franklin Delano Roosevelt was commemorated by the original signatories to the United Nations Charter in 1945.

The image remains vivid in my mind—my stout grandfather, poly-cotton shirt tucked tightly into the belted slacks wrapped high around his paunch, a small, bespectacled gnome beside these towering giants. *Adaiyappa*, he exclaims, looking up at trunks bearing several hundred cubic meters of solid hardwood. "How many millions of rupees, these trees!"

I was unnerved. I knew of distant relations who had traded in the last of the timber from the now-denuded Andaman Islands, and of others who were said to have pioneered the creation of the wretched single-use plastic sachets of soap and shampoo littering the edges of most Indian roadways. South of Chennai, my own mother's father was helping to fill in a tract of wetlands cherished by birdwatchers, hoping to build an apartment complex or a shopping mall.

All of this I knew. But still, having come to these northern Californian groves with Ayya, hoping to share with him some of the wonder I had felt at their stark and seemingly immovable mass, I was flustered by the ease with which he had already converted their physical bulk into money. I can't recall now how I reacted to what he said, or what I said in return, if anything at all. But I do remember that whatever we saw together in those few days, what first caught his notice was the price of purchase on these things, even if they were no more than secondhand knickknacks lying for sale on the lawns of nearby houses.

At the time, I was studying for my PhD at UC Berkeley. After food and rent, I spent most of the rest of my stipend on books. Proper bookshelves would have been expensive, and so I'd bought a few planks of wood from a local "eco-timber" shop and stacked them between eight cheap concrete cinderblocks against one wall of my room.

Ayya was impressed, with my thrift and with the number of books I'd already gathered for my studies. He described those few modest shelves proudly to others as my "library" and would often ask, whenever we spoke in the coming years, how my library was. Meanwhile, he was constantly downplaying how much he had read or learned himself. "What do I know anyway?" he would ask my mother at the dinner table in Los Angeles. "I'm an unlettered man."

My difficulty with Ayya's reaction to those redwood trees had much to do with what I was reading at the time from the shelves that my grandfather admired so much. I was learning to think critically about the history of modern capitalism: the accumulation of profit through exploitation, the ravaging of environments in the name of development, the colonial dispossession of native populations, the way that certain classes of colonized people always found a way to profit themselves from such exploitation, destruction, and domination. Here was my own grandfather, a merchant from a market town in south India, who had earned his living by taking a margin on things always grown and made by others, never by himself.

In his many stories about his various trading ventures, I am struck by how casually Ayya refers to so many different kinds of things with just one Tamil word, *sarakku*, goods. It is indeed as though everything is fundamentally equivalent when it comes to business: everything has a price, a value fixed in money terms, and the only question is how much that thing could be bought or sold for at any given moment, in relation to other things and other moments.

There are also those various tricks that Ayya admits in this game of assigning a favorable price to things, casual lies that confirm the picture we often have of the immoral merchant. Although Ayya is candid now about these lies, I'm not sure that he regrets having told them. As he has often said, with rueful conviction, he could not have raised his eight children without lying and cheating.

None of this, however, seems to have compromised his reputation in the markets in which he worked. Ayya insists that it was his *vilasam,* the good name of his enterprise, that drew more buyers and sellers than he could handle, decade after decade. His vivid stories of business in some of the most tumultuous decades of the twentieth century give a compelling sense of market relations as social and moral relations, based on fragile ties of trust, dependence, and anticipation.

In spite of the many deceits built into these transactions, they carry a moral charge that distinguishes good businessmen from others in all the many senses of this simple word, "good." I think such morality is expressed in practices as routine as the naming of debts as *patru*—literally, connection, relation, or attachment in Tamil—in the daily account books that Ayya and his fellow businessmen would keep. *Patru* build business relationships only insofar as these debts are repaid. *Patru,* that is, record the relations of mutual dependence and trust that are built through the trading of debts.

Talk about markets these days inevitably brings reflections on globalization, as market relations appear to draw, for better or for worse, distant places ever closer to each other. Ayya's stories remind us that there are long histories of global exchange, dependence, and development that underpin what we identify now with this particular idea. Recall, for example, Ayya's profound image of New York City newspaper pages arriving by ship in Rangoon, reused as packaging material but also yielding a glimpse of events convulsing the world in the 1930s.

Or, consider the effects of global depression on agrarian and market relations in Burma at this time, as Ayya describes them from his vantage point as a small trader in Okpo. Recall the Chinese and Japanese goods he sold from there, the Burmese earnings and commodities exported then to India, or the fruit from America, Australia, and Afghanistan that Ayya later sold in Madurai. Vast worlds of traffic come into focus in the details of a single life.

There is much to be learned by following the movement of such goods, as I came to see myself in the 1980s as we flew back and forth across the Pacific Ocean, American children taken by our parents back to an India we hardly knew. In those years before India's economic liberalization, we sat beside young men trafficking in televisions, refrigerators, and stereo systems between Singapore and Madras. The back aisles of those planes were always thick with their cigarette smoke, and there were rumors about the gold, diamonds, and other valuables smuggled into India within these spacious devices.

We came ourselves with bursting bundles of Samsonite, loaded with single-use syringes, throwaway razors, Ziploc bags, and other eminently disposable items. And those who received them would devise ways of maintaining these American goods until the next round of visitors arrived.

One afternoon not long ago in Madurai, Ayya and I watched the video recording of our trip together to Burma in 2002. Senthi Chithappa and

Nirmala Chithi, my aunt and uncle who have cared tirelessly and selflessly for Ayya all these years, also sat before the television with us in the house they shared in Anna Nagar. Ten years had passed, and the footage was grainy, often interrupted by the deterioration of the videocassette. But in other ways, it seemed as though there was hardly a moment dividing that time from this one. We realized with a shock that Ayya was wearing the same striped green T-shirt this afternoon that he wore in the video from 2002, and the same pair of clip-on sunglass lenses were clipped to his eyeglasses even now.

All of this created a kind of telescoping effect, so that it became difficult to distinguish Ayya then from Ayya now. At the sight of him on-screen picking his way down the scrubby railway embankment to the site of his father's grave, my uncle suddenly said "carefully, carefully," almost to himself, but also to Ayya, as if that elderly man in the video was the very man seated beside us, as if he was tentatively taking those steps right now.

There was something profound in this confusion. It reminded us of how tenaciously Ayya maintained his identity over many passing years and how deeply he still carried with him the promise of a Burmese life led seventy years ago.

In our family, Ayya's grandfather may have been the first to go to Burma. Some say that he had carried sacks of salt to earn his living. Ayya's own story begins with the mystery of his birthplace: in Tamil Nadu perhaps, or somewhere in Burma instead. Sailing with his father to Rangoon at the age of thirteen, he spent nearly a decade of his life in the small town of Okpo, ninety-five miles north of the capital along the railway line to Prome. His depiction of those years is vivid: the daily life of their provisions store and their familial and commercial networks throughout the region and back to India. We learn that most of Ayya's friends at that time were Burmese and that they knew him both as Mariappa and as Maung Chit Pyon.

In the 1930s, mounting economic and social tensions culminated in anti-Indian communal riots in Rangoon and other localities. Indian migrants and settlers were the most visible faces of the colonial domination of Burma. As the value of Burmese rice exports plummeted during the global economic depression of the 1930s, Chettiar moneylenders from Tamil Nadu gained control of over 3 million acres of paddy fields in the lowlands of the

Irawaddy delta. Although Ayya conveys a gripping sense of the broader social tensions building at that time, his descriptions retain an idyllic fullness. "I lived as a Burmese man with other Burmese," he says.

It is almost as if the looming threat of the war hangs over every moment of these stories, deepening their hues of hope and satisfaction. We always knew, or so we thought, that Ayya had walked from Burma to India at the outbreak of the Second World War. Over the passing years, the twists and turns of a precarious 1,700-mile journey by rail, boat, steamer, bullock cart, and foot had been contracted to its most dangerous and difficult stage: the 110-mile trek through the jungles of the Arakan mountains down to the Burmese fishing village of Taungup.

Ayya and his elder brother Mutharasu left Okpo soon after the first Japanese air raids on Rangoon in December 1941. His account of the trek is particularly harrowing, describing the stony faces with which they greeted all those begging them for drinking water along the way and the heaps of nameless bodies beside which they cooked and slept each night. There was the sheer fact of their own survival, but there were also acts of betrayal that haunted him for many years.

Historian Hugh Tinker, who served in 1942 with an Indian Army unit operating near another evacuation route from Upper Burma, has called this exodus of Indians from Burma a "forgotten long march," barely acknowledged in the archives of history. Tinker's account would place my grandfather among at least 400,000 refugees seeking overland passage to India, taking three successive routes across different frontier zones as Japanese armies advanced north through the months of 1942. Although the number of casualties will never be known, somewhere between 10,000 and 50,000 of them likely died, succumbing to dysentery, smallpox, malaria, and cholera.

Casualties appear to have run this high in part because of official meanness and indifference. Indian workers—needed in Rangoon to tend the city and to work shipping docks still receiving war supplies—were dissuaded from fleeing in the first months of fighting, turned back from evacuation routes, denied available supplies, and otherwise left to fend for themselves. Along the 110-mile Arakan jungle route that Ayya had followed along with 100,000 to 200,000 other refugees, there was a single British officer, from the Forest Service, on hand to attempt necessary aid.

There are some literary representations, in Tamil and other languages, of the flight of Indians from Burma. There is also the well-known depiction of these events in the 1952 Tamil film *Parasakti*. Three Tamil brothers lead a prosperous life in Rangoon, the spire of the Shwedagon Pagoda visible from the open window of their home. Then the war comes, interrupting their life and complicating their flight. Japanese bombers shell a column of refugees on foot, and in a tidy hospital bunker with compassionate doctors on duty, Chandrasekaran learns of the likely death of his brother Gnanase-karan. Meanwhile, the ship that Gunasekaran takes to see his sister in India is stranded at sea, and when he finally arrives in Madras, he finds himself utterly bereft of sympathy, care, respect, or even water. From the standpoint of Ayya's recollections, what is most peculiar about these scenes is the way that they reverse his narrative of neglect and care. Ayya had arrived in India to great fanfare, but only after having survived gruesome conditions of heedless suffering and neglect along the way.

Ayya describes how he and his brother made their way from the Burmese coast to Chittagong, and then to Calcutta, Madras, and ultimately Pudur. He had left almost everything behind in Okpo, unsure of when he might return. He could not have guessed that this would happen sixty years later, in 2002, when my father and I took Ayya back to investigate what remained of his former life there.

As we waited for our flight to Yangon (Rangoon) in a posh Singapore airport lounge, he described his first steamship voyage across the Bay of Bengal. Much had changed. A copy of the Lonely Planet Myanmar tourist guide now rested on his lap as we spoke. Printed in white block letters on one corner of the cover was a question posed with the ruling military junta in mind: "Should you go?"

Waiting for us in Yangon were the children and grandchildren of Ayya's uncle Muthiah Nadar, whom the war had failed to dislodge. In spite of the tremendous hardship of several decades of life under military rule, we could see the vibrant and extraordinary forms of cultural commingling that had also transpired here. We still had ties of kinship with many families in Yangon and other nearby towns, and it seemed that every house we visited was founded on a different kind of marital alliance and a unique form of religious faith.

My most vivid impression of those visits was the juxtaposition of two large framed photographs, side-by-side, on the wall of one of those houses: one of Aung San, leader of Burma's own movement for independence from Britain, and the other of K. Kamaraj, former chief minister of Tamil Nadu and one of the most famous scions of the Nadar caste.

Muthiah Nadar's children lavished Ayya with their affections and led us along the highway north of Yangon, songs from the 1971 Hindi film *Hare Krishna Hare Ram* blaring from our white minivan's open windows. Okpo was quiet. As we walked along the broad, packed-dirt road bisecting the center of town, men and women cycled past us, wide-brimmed hats and umbrellas shielding them from the morning sun. Although we found my great-grandfather's tomb, there was no trace of that iron box and its clues into the circumstances of Ayya's birth.

The flight from Burma was the pivotal event of Ayya's life, the lodestone to which he would always turn when making sense of his experience—to this day, he hasn't settled his accounts with that country and its people. But, he was only twenty-two when he returned to India as a refugee. Life began again in Pudur, with other goods, other kin, and the one person with whom he had traded the most over the years—my grandmother Paati.

Some years back, there was something that Ayya wanted me to read. It was a short story from the Tamil weekly magazine *Ananda Vikatan*, part of what would later become Tamil writer Vairamuthu's *Kallikattu Ithikasam*. In a small market town, picking out jewelry for his daughter's upcoming marriage, Peya Thevar gets news of his wife's sudden death. As his bullock cart slowly trundles back to his village, where Alagamma lies within the mud-walled house they had built together, he is overwhelmed by images of the forty-five years of marriage they shared.

Once, Peya Thevar recalls, he had wrestled her to the ground of a millet field they were harvesting in silence. They had been fighting and hadn't slept together or even talked for three long years. Alagamma had spotted a snake sliding close to Peya Thevar's back as they lay there together, Vairamuthu writes, but so focused was her passion that she had grabbed and held it firmly by the neck, heaving it over the stalks of millet only after she had pushed aside her spent and weary man.

I remember Ayya sitting beside me, looking keenly while I read this story to myself. "Do you understand?" he asked me twice, perhaps with my limited experience of Tamil in mind, perhaps with my limited experience of life instead. What could I say? I understood enough to be both moved and embarrassed by what he had given me. I was twenty-eight years old, far from marriage, far from anyone I'd ever loved.

Later, he said that what he wanted to show me was the story's beautiful depiction of the countryside and rural livelihood. But the moment itself stayed with me like a small jewel to tuck away and marvel at secretly, glimmering with the kinds of feelings that my grandparents might have kept to themselves while Paati was still alive.

Hour by hour, at every pause between the writing of these words, what resurfaces in my mind is a scratchy recording of Paati's voice from 1973, singing for a distant grandchild she had never met. She had cried for over a week when my father and mother first left for New York in 1972. "For one full week," she later said to my mother's parents, "I couldn't eat, I couldn't do anything. How my hands and feet shook and trembled without my knowing it, on the day that Ganesan left."

Ayya and Paati were grateful for the letters and photos that were posted regularly back to Madurai. But their replies by mail made plaintive descriptions of various ailments and repeated appeals for medical advice. They had two sons and one son-in-law who were doctors, all three of whom were permanently settled by 1980 in the United States, far from their aging parents as well as the country that had financed their medical education. Ayya was always wary of making stark pronouncements about such things. Paati was fiercely loyal to her children but nevertheless unconditional in her judgment. This was a case of betrayal.

Quarrels between Ayya and Paati came often. Sometimes, these exchanges were quite funny. Paati would bring a glass of tea for Ayya. "What *di* is this?" Ayya would ask, using a disrespectfully casual Tamil word addressed to women and scowling at the taste of what she'd brought him. "What, you address me this insultingly, as *di*?" Paati would snap. "I asked what *tea* is this," Ayya would answer, trying to handle the situation deftly.

Other times, day after day would pass in tense silence with neither willing to give in to the other. Ayya was hardly audible in Paati's company, as some of his own stories here imply. Household conversations revolved around her forceful opinions and emphatic assertions while she held court among her children, daughters-in-law, and visiting houseguests, and even after she had retreated out of sight and earshot.

This transcribed excerpt from one conversation I had with Ayya helps me imagine how quarrels between them might have gone:

Ayya: Paati and I would often fight, no?
Anand: Really?
Ayya: Yes.
Anand: Often?
Ayya: Yes . . . The fights would come for all kinds of reasons.
Anand: Tell me about something that happened.
Ayya: (laughs)
Anand: Tell me, tell me something that happened, just tell me . . .
Ayya: She . . . She had a lot of saris. I'd bought a lot of silk saris for her. "I don't have this kind," she'd say whenever we went to a shop.
Anand: "Not this kind," what do you mean by that?
Ayya: "I don't have a sari with this design" . . . She'd want to buy this. I'd refuse.
Anand: Mmm . . .
Ayya: Then of course we'd fight.
Anand: Mmm . . . Wouldn't you also feel this way? "I don't have a shirt with this design . . . I don't have slippers with this design . . ."
Ayya: For me, two or three pairs of slippers were enough.
Anand: Mmm . . .
Ayya: They still come with so many slippers. I throw them all away . . .
Anand: Mmm . . .
Ayya: Or I give them to someone else.
Anand: Mmm . . .
Ayya: I don't like too much of anything. But Paati . . . Handbags, for example . . .
Anand: What?
Ayya: Handbags.
Anand: Oh, handbags . . .
Ayya: When she died, do you know how many she had?
Anand: I don't know!
Ayya: She probably had fifty handbags.
Anand: (laughs)
Ayya: And so fights would come, no?
Anand: How would you handle that?
Ayya: If they came, what to do? Might as well try to make my peace. I needed her too, no?
Anand: Mmm . . .

Although they often disagreed, and despite the disdainful remarks that Ayya sometimes makes about her here, my grandparents were equals in intelligence, resolve, and judgment. They carried on like this for over fifty years. And once in awhile, those around them also caught a glimpse of the love that grew out of their quarrels. Here, for example, is the most indelible impression that I have of the life they shared: Ayya, dazed, being wheeled out of an operating room where he had just lost his prostate gland, and Paati, rushing to walk alongside him, struggling to keep up in the thick folds of her sari, saying something to him that I was too far away to hear, but with more care and concern playing on her face than I had ever seen before.

Paati had already begun chemotherapy again for the cancer in her breast, which had returned after a mastectomy five years earlier. She was wearing a blue beret to cover her bare head and a thick sweater to defend against the cold of the hospital. Back in Los Angeles myself then, just after college, I tended to Ayya for a few weeks, dressing his wounds as he recuperated from the surgery. Then Paati and Ayya traveled back to India with me in April 1995.

They were both in delicate shape, but our greatest cause for alarm came when Ayya wandered off by himself down one of the long terminal halls in Singapore. We found him just minutes before our connection to Madras. Ayya was nonchalant, Paati furious.

For nearly two more years, Paati survived her long illness. And then, as Ayya tells it, there was nothing to do but to bear what came.

In many ways, this book is a consequence of what Ayya became in Paati's absence. In the years that followed her death, there was a certain picture of his life that gained sharpness and definition, the idea of his life as a moral example. Offering praise as a means of consolation, many of those around him turned the quirks of his experience into simple moral precepts and examples that others could also follow.

We were all reminded endlessly of his history, called on to learn from this history, told of principles that we also ought to follow out of respect to this history. Even Ayya said something like this in the letter that he wrote me a few months after Paati's death. "I've lived in this world now for 77 years," he'd written toward the end of that letter. "I haven't suffered very much in these days of my life. But I've toiled a lot. What I want is for my children, grandsons, and granddaughters to live by my principles."

I've tried many times to imagine Ayya writing this letter, filling out the last bit of space on the aerogram's small overleaf with these reflections on the character of his life. Why did he insist that he hadn't suffered very much, after having lost his wife? Why suddenly mention the extent of his toils? What were these principles that he wanted the rest of us to live by?

Ayya had just survived Paati, and he was already looking ahead to his place in a world that would survive him in turn. But there was nothing straightforward in this vision of a legacy. Ayya had always insisted that he had nothing to teach, that everyone else should live as they wanted to live. What then remained to be learned from his experience?

It is difficult to obtain such insights into anyone's life, even someone you might know as well as your own grandfather. You can ask people what they think is most important to do. They will often say it, too. Work hard. Study well. Don't lie. Be generous. Control your desires. It's very easy to invoke such principles when we talk about what it means to lead a good life.

Much more difficult, however, is to try to understand how these ideas come to shape the way in which people actually live, day to day and moment to moment. Ask a lot of questions, listen patiently to whatever answers come in return, and still, things happen all the time that come completely by surprise. These things become visible only when you immerse yourself in the time and space of people's lives, when you pay attention to details as small as daily habits and routines.

I was stunned, for example, when I first learned that Ayya counted his steps as he walked each morning. It was a simple thing, just a habit folded into a daily routine. Still, it was something that I'd never imagined him doing, although I'd walked these same streets with him countless times until then. It was like a sudden opening into the depth of a life.

Everyone knew that there were certain things that Ayya added up zealously: the costs of various household things, streams of income and expenditure, the rates of return that made some investments of time and money more attractive than others. Whenever I took an auto rickshaw back to the house in Anna Nagar, I would ask the auto driver to park a little farther down the street, away from the house, to avoid an inevitably embarrassing scene: Ayya coming out angrily to challenge the driver on the rate that we had agreed on, convinced that the man was taking advantage of his American grandson for speaking like a stranger in Madurai.

I knew that Ayya had been gifted at arithmetic even as a child. I knew that he relied on his counting skills in all the decades that he did business. I knew that even now, he totaled up the cost and value of the smallest things. Still, despite all of this, the notion that Ayya counted even the beats of his stick against the street as he walked was something extraordinary.

He did this, he said, to keep his mind on the present, to keep his attention focused on each step as he took it, so that he wouldn't trip up on rocks or potholes in the road. The counting, in other words, was a technique to keep in health, to keep on living, to maintain a rhythm of daily life that carried onward from moment to moment, day to day. I found myself wondering how deep this went. In the quiet of his mind, was he always counting? When else, how else, did he rely on these numbers? Here was a glimpse of an essential dimension of his practical life.

Ayya's *ulaippu*, his toil, also seems to have this very practical significance that reaches across so many different things he does. To be sure, he'd always worked long and diligent hours, as most everyone who knows him has observed. But look at how that lifetime of hard work has shaped the most basic ways in which he confronts the uncertainties of time. Toil is a way of acting now with future consequences foremost in mind, a way of reminding oneself always of how consequences accumulate, even one coin at a time, as Ayya says.

I think again, for example, of that green T-shirt he still often wears, the one he'd worn that day in 2002 when we visited Okpo. There's now an uneven line of stitching below that T-shirt's pocket, which Ayya had stitched himself when the pocket gave way some years ago. "Keep it carefully," he said, when I took a picture of these threads on a shirt that was now twenty years old. "Put it in this book even," he added, "to show how Ayya lived." Once again, the ethical principle was best understood as a practical way of approaching ordinary life.

The more I think about Ayya's life, the more it seems that so much of what he's done has been shaped by habits of transaction developed in various market environments. The simplest name for these principles is *kodukkal-vaangal* or "giving-and-taking," and it occurs with remarkable consistency throughout these varied stories. In the bazaar, Ayya says, he always promptly paid others what they were owed and never took more than he could repay. But look at how he recalls other spaces and situations that might seem to have very little to do with such transactions: the son he gave instead of money toward the Indo-Chinese war, or the unease he felt, as a cancer patient, in taking more blood than he'd given in the midst of a surgery.

Even in the case of this book, Ayya worries that people may come uninvited to heap praise upon him, creating debts that he would then have to repay. "I never take what others give for free," he tells me.

Of course this isn't entirely true. Now more than ever before, my grandfather depends upon the charity and generosity of his children. But still, in the biggest and smallest of ways, Ayya has always sought to balance his accounts and to maintain, day by day, the value of his name and reputation. These were the concerns that kept him awake each night for decades, compulsively totaling the balance of each of his individual transactions. And these are the concerns that we ought to keep in mind when we try to grapple with the "lessons of experience" that Ayya describes as the substance of his education.

There is nothing fated or inevitable in the world as Ayya depicts it, nothing that is meant to go one way or another. Things are far more open than we want or hope, and what we learn through experience is how to deal effectively with such surprises when they come. Principles are nothing more than these small techniques, ways that we may learn simply to live with the unexpected—like counting your steps, for example, to pay attention to the rocks beneath your feet.

January 15, 2012. I'm hunched over my laptop in one corner of the living room in Anna Nagar, organizing the audio recordings of some of the dialogues we have had over the last week. Ayya is in his chair, heels at rest on a table and the Lonely Planet Burma guidebook on his knee for support, writing on a pad of lined paper. It's the morning of the annual Tamil Pongal festival, but I've paid little attention to this.

Ayya, meanwhile, seems to have forgotten that the festival began today. "Look," he tells me. "All these things from so long ago that I've been remembering, but I've forgotten even this fact about today."

My aunt Meena comes by the house with her family. Neither Ayya nor I notice at first. I remain engrossed in my laptop and headphones; Ayya remains engaged in his writing. "Ayya hasn't bathed yet? Is he that absorbed in this work?" Meena Athai asks Nirmala Chithi. "Both of them, this is all they've been doing," my aunt replies.

After some time, Ayya gives me what he's written. What I see brings a big laugh bursting from somewhere deep within my chest. It's brilliant. Ayya has turned the tables, balanced the accounts, cleared his debts for all the work that I've been doing on his behalf. Until now, I had been working to give an account of his life. But now he's also given, for the book, his own brief account of my life in turn—the words that close this book.

It was the final morning of a weeklong trip to India. A weeklong trip from America to this one house in Anna Nagar, that is, to try to pull together the materials for the Tamil edition of this book. Back in the summer of 2008, I had sat with Ayya over many days in Madurai and Chennai, asking a series of questions about his life and recording what he'd said. Although, as an anthropologist, I'd had such conversations with countless older men and women in India and elsewhere, it took awhile to figure out how best to do fieldwork with my own grandfather.

Transcripts of those first few dialogues were very much like the exchange that appeared a few pages earlier: his recollections, observations, and opinions came in small bits and pieces, mixed up with my own questions, nudges, and other vocal expressions of interest and encouragement. At first, Ayya felt compelled to speak in very formal Tamil, and he kept tripping up on the grammar of these complicated sentences. I encouraged him to speak as he usually does, and the conversation began to flow.

Still, Ayya was not someone used to holding an audience captive with long and elaborate stories. He wasn't inclined to linger on every detail of any moment or event, or to heighten or deepen the drama as gifted storytellers do. And so in our conversations about his life, I was an incessant, insistent, interruptive presence.

Later, the Tamil writer Kamalalayan helped shape these dialogues into narratives, as we worked closely together on the first Tamil edition of this book. Over the course of many months, back and forth by phone and e-mail between Chennai and Baltimore, he and I arranged these scattered exchanges into blocs of narrative, these blocs into stories, and these stories into chapters of a book. A separate challenge later arose when it came to the English edition of this project, as I tried to find a way of translating everything that Ayya had said in colloquial Tamil into a voice that wasn't his, and yet could have been.

I had come to Madurai that January with a very rough and fragmentary Tamil draft in hand and a long list of doubts and questions in mind. Once again, Ayya and I spoke for many, many hours. There were certain times each day when we could do this in a focused manner: after meals, for example, and after he'd taken some rest. Most of the time, however, we had to work with the needs and limits of his body in mind, as well as with the pulls and pressures of his familial and social world.

Even in these circumstances, I found that there were endless occasions for small snippets of dialogue, a few seconds or a couple of minutes of his thoughts to record as we walked, ate, or relaxed together. His memory was like a deep and moody sea that would suddenly advance upon us when we didn't expect it, stranding new treasures on the sand each time the waters receded. It was best to have my digital voice recorder always ready.

Feelings also ebbed and flowed with our conversation, shaping what we found. Ayya took very seriously the work that we were doing together. "OK, let's go back to our work," he would say, whenever he wanted to begin our discussions once more. "Ask," he'd often insist, as if acknowledging that these questions were essential in dredging the depths of what he could recall. Sometimes, he would suddenly erupt in anger and frustration at my ceaseless prodding for clarity and detail. "Enough! I've said all that! You're asking that same question again and again, like some lawyer."

But just as suddenly, a question could create an unexpected opening. His face would soften into a smile, his eyes would slowly close for a few seconds, and he would drift off into a vivid story about some other event or situation I'd never heard about.

In the midst of all this, something else unexpected and extraordinary started to happen. Ayya, who had never kept a journal or diary himself, also began to write for the book. At first there were minor cuts and corrections he made to the working draft that was lying on the table. Then he began to add a few handwritten lines in the margins of my printout. And then on that morning of January 15, Ayya modestly asked whether he could write a few pages himself.

I was elated. He was a retired fruit merchant in Madurai, I was a university professor in the United States, and we'd been working closely with a freelance writer and former factory machinist who lived just outside of Chennai. We were unlikely collaborators. And yet, we were writing a book together.

"Storytelling is always the art of repeating stories, and this art is lost when the stories are no longer retained," wrote the German Jewish literary scholar Walter Benjamin. These words help me understand why Ayya may have started to think much more about his own life as a story when he began to face his own mortality. They also give a sense of why he may have shared this story as something for his grandchildren, great-grandchildren, and other descendants yet to come. Individual stories may be lost, but with this loss comes a more troubling threat: loss of the very means of making sense of experience.

I think that Ayya may be less concerned about the forgetting of his stories than the forgetting of the arts they represent: arts of experience, ways of relying upon the accumulating lessons of life in order to handle the unexpected demands of the present and future. It's the possible survival of such arts of living that has drawn both of us ever deeper into this book.

What happens then when such a life becomes a public artifact? We glimpsed an answer to this question in September 2012, when the Tamil edition of this project was launched in Madurai. Ayya's person began to spread and proliferate into infinite echoes of himself.

There was the book itself—copies suddenly heaped up in piles on the very tables where we had drafted it, volumes that Ayya himself could pick up and examine as expressions of his life. There were the reporters who dropped by the house with plans to place him into other printed sheaves. Then there were images like the photograph of Ayya walking in blue shorts and a striped T-shirt, which I had taken one morning on the street outside the house.

This outline of my grandfather walking began to migrate and multiply in wildly unpredictable ways: onto the cover of the Tamil edition, onto the

# மிச்சம் மீதி

### ஓர் அனுபவக் கணக்கு

எம்.பி. மாரியப்பன்
ஆனந்த் பாண்டியன்
தொகுப்பும் மொழிபெயர்ப்பும்
கமலாலயன்

posters and invitations for the book launch, onto some unknown beach adorning the front of a T-shirt made for all of Ayya's grandchildren, even onto a mug dropped anonymously at the house one morning, on which Ayya was seen striding across a cornucopia of fruit with the acclamation "O righteous balance scale . . ." Suddenly, in the argot of these times, Ayya himself had become a meme.

The book launch itself took place one Saturday evening, on the rooftop of a small hotel across the road from the American College in Madurai. Many of Ayya's living relatives were packed into that hall. There were people I knew from my own fieldwork in the area, but also many faces that I didn't recognize. I remember catching a glimpse of one man who'd come in bare feet, from where I have no idea. The event had been advertised in the local papers that day, and throughout the evening, it kept tilting between a public discussion and a family affair.

Many of the speakers digested moral lessons to follow from Ayya's stories. Someone described how he had lost himself in the events of my grandfather's life: "As I saw all this happen, I became Mariappa Nadar myself." Someone else identified with the grandson in the story, ruing the loss of his own grandmother's tales. N. Muthumohan, a professor at Madurai Kamaraj University, gave an artful exegesis of the entire text by lingering on the nuances of a single line: "I was the first to show Anand the light of the sun."

I can see how all of us that day were circling around the same question in various ways: why pay such close attention to the life of someone so ordinary, so unknown? Novelist and Tamil public intellectual Su. Venkatesan, who had written a profound foreword for the Tamil edition, posed this question most bluntly in his remarks: "What is there, in this book about M. P. Mariappan, for those of us who don't belong to his family?"

In all the time that I've worked on this project, this problem has troubled me continually. It's a problem that cuts to the heart of anthropology, to the way we often tend in this field to work with such idiosyncratic people, places, and situations. Is our work meant for those who are already familiar with these situations? What is there to learn for those who have never gone to these places and never intend to do so? How do larger insights grow from such detailed accounts of individuals whom our readers will never otherwise meet?

Venkatesan went on to say something remarkable that evening in Madurai, offering up an answer of his own to his question about the book: "All his life, this grandfather has been tallying up accounts. But sitting right next to him, this grandson has been tallying up his grandfather's life. The grandfather is someone who has always held onto the pans of a balance scale. But here is someone who has put him onto the pan of one of those scales!" All of us laughed, as my friend knew we would.

Two sets of ledgers, two sets of scales. One might easily be imagined as the master of the other: the anthropologist weighs the weigher at work. The image, however, is also a scene of apprenticeship: a lesson in a way of life, the sharing of a mode of accounting, the passing onward of a habit of reckoning, from one practical world into another.

Any account, whether a business ledger or a story to tell, is far more than a recounting of what has already happened. An account is also an invitation to nurture a relationship—a way of making unfamiliar persons and things familiar to each other, a trail of transactions through a world of experience, an image of a possible world in common.

You may object to the terms that an account uses to record what happens. You may reject the values that it assigns to various acts and things, or the obligations and responsibilities that it pegs to those things. Still, traders skilled with tales and goods will persuade you to stay by their side. They will make you ask questions about how you've gotten to that place. And they will leave you, for better or worse, with aspirations you never thought to kindle.

Traders like my grandfather work with many temptations. One of the most powerful among them is hope. Hope is something easy to dismiss as flimsy, fickle, even naive. It's difficult to say where hope comes from and whether its presence is even warranted by the circumstances where we find it. Hope is, however, a quality essential to the momentum of these times, to the immense and unimaginable movement of modern lives such as Ayya's.

We often take hope as a desire for something specific: this or that object to long and wish for. But one of the most profound lessons of Ayya's life, I think, concerns the pull of hope even in the absence of such clarity. Think of it as a current sweeping from an unknown source to an unforeseeable destination—think of what has happened with this book, with the person at its heart, with the lives of so many others like and unlike him.

Hope is not a private or a personal feeling, a currency tucked into the pockets of the optimistic, devout, or ambitious alone. It's something more diffuse, a feeling in the world at large, a momentum that ebbs and flows with the texture of interwoven lives. "The anxieties of hope," anthropologist Michael Jackson has written, "spring from the fundamentally unstable and ambiguous nature of our relationships with others and with the world."

Ayya may be right that no one could have had, or should have wanted, a life such as his. Aspirations for the future take many contradictory paths, in modern India as elsewhere. I think of this book's hope as something other than a call for emulation: less a settling of accounts with my grandfather, that is, than an embrace of their unsettled nature.

Let's head to the bazaar then, to look for Ayya and see what he has on hand today. Just one warning—try to count along with him, and keep track of what he writes down in those ledgers of his. He's a tricky one, that Ayya of ours.

ᔄ

# AFTERWORD

VEENA DAS

This book was born through the joint labors of an aging grandfather and his grandson, an anthropologist, bursting with curiosity about what a life such as that of his grandfather Ayya might mean, and for whom it might be written. Ayya in Tamil means "father"—an appellation that stuck to the protagonist of this story when his little grandson addressed him thus by mimicking his own father's term for him. Thus, the title already hints that the voice of the grandson is not only that of the adult anthropologist but also that of the child.

The origin of the project lies in what Ayya describes as a stray thought, but when it was voiced—"When will you write *my* story?"—it took on the force of a claim that could not be denied. The result is a stunning book in which a grandfather and a grandson each learn who the other is through the other's words, but not, however, in a symmetrical fashion. Braided into the stark simplicity of the book are many other voices—present and absent—that define its texture.

Let us ask: what is the book's idea of itself? It is not a confessional text written in the form of self-examination, in which one strives to discover the truth about oneself. Anand Pandian thinks of the book as a memoir and alludes to other memoirs and life histories within anthropology. For Ayya, "Anand has fulfilled that stray thought of mine, of Mariappan's. Mariappan . . . Born to some poor soul, he wandered around all over the place, and now here he is, sitting on this soil, talking to his grandson." These sentences, in the act of telling, move the narrator from the use of first person (these are how things are with me) to the third person (an impersonal witness of life) from where he can see the journey that Mariappan's life was.

So the best way to think of this book might be as a legacy, a last will and testament, witness to a life that Ayya wants his descendants to know. But it is also a witness to the stupendous changes that took place in the caste to which Ayya belonged, in the political systems of the nations in which he tried to make his home, and to the way aspirations changed as each generation tried to make a different future for itself. As Anand says, "No life is small as it might appear from a distance. Vast worlds lie buried within the smallest details of ordinary life."

The importance of looking at a single life, a singularity, is that it can show how forces contingent and structural, from pasts known and unknown, can come together to define a life—not lives in general but life in its singularity. Ayya's story itself would be enough to challenge the idea that in "traditional societies" a person can be taken as the "average man" or that one person's experience can stand for anyone's experience. Such ideas allow the story of modernity to be told as if it were synonymous with the advent of human freedom in society. Yet, the actual experience of historical individuals shows that such a story functions more as the ideology of social science than as a description of actual social formations.

In my brief afterword, I want to draw attention to two aspects of the book that function as a signature of Ayya's life. The first is the way that tropes of the market, of giving and receiving, of credits and debts, run through the text and color its social relations. The second is the poverty of words through which powerful emotions are sometimes kept at bay in the narration. At times these two aspects combine to create the picture of an austere life; at other times one is left with a sense of the suffocation that may have overcome Ayya as he struggled to claim the experience of grief at the losses that punctuate his life.

Ayya's childhood seems as if it were spent in a trance. He registers stories of the humiliations heaped on the Nadar caste to which he belonged: no water from upper caste houses for thirsty travelers in case their touch polluted the pot; not a shirt for Ayya, nor slippers either. It is not entirely clear from his account whether all Nadars suffered from the same humiliations or whether Ayya's experience was a result of poverty, an often absent father and a lower caste status that marked his case in particular. Yet this was also a period of tremendous social mobilization as the Nadar caste association set up schools and colleges where children of the caste could study. Ayya discovered early his brilliance at arithmetic but its importance for him would only be revealed later when he moved to Burma with his father and learned the arts of trading. Otherwise, he seems to have been a spectator to events that forcefully ripped apart his life again and again.

There are fences around what must have been some of Ayya's most profound experiences, such as those of death, abandonment, and betrayal. Consider that his mother died when Ayya was in the third grade, but he could not recall any feeling of sadness: "I didn't know or understand anything back then. You may not believe this, but I wasn't even sad. I didn't feel anything although Amma had just left us all behind." The only way the event registered then was in the happiness of receiving new clothes as traditional funerary gifts from the mother's relatives. Yet the grief must have become part of who he was, for years later, when he is holding a newborn granddaughter, he says that it is his mother come back to him.

Even in the eighth grade when his family was banished from the caste and he was expelled from school due to the rowdy behavior of his uncle, he says, "at that age you do not know what you have lost." His two young sisters were growing by his side but with no one to dress them—they just tied strips of cloth torn from their deceased mother's saris around their waists. This too, as he remembers it, evoked little response or concern. Was this because this was knowledge too difficult to bear, or because his sisters already belonged to a different feminine world against which he found himself fenced off?

Much later when Ayya's own daughter, married to the son of one of these sisters, died, the connection between the sisters who could not go out of the house because they did not have clothes and the daughter who died under mysterious circumstances appears to have remained elusive to Ayya. In the face of loss, words appear to choke him. Only when his own wife of many long years of trials and tribulations dies, does he admit to tears flowing unchecked, dreams coming unbidden, and, with the urge to go on visiting her at the hospital, having to be reminded that she was dead: "Even now when I think of Paati, tears come unbidden to my eyes. I cried when my father died. In the sixty-three years since his time had come, only now do my eyes flood by themselves like this. This too will stop in a few days, I think."

It seems that grief is not necessarily a good teacher and that Ayya, who is so good otherwise in drawing lessons from both successes and failures, cannot find words for the disappearance of these women from his world. So these unbidden tears with a gap of sixty-three years must do his speaking for him.

The vocabulary that comes most easily to Ayya is the vocabulary of the bazaar—counting and recounting, credit and debt, buying and selling, commission and interest. It is with this vocabulary that he carves out a moral life. Thus, for instance, he could not bear the way simple peasants were fooled into buying inferior cloth in his father-in-law's shop, where he was an assistant, and so he left to become a trader in fruit. Repeatedly, he registers his discomfort at the way in which fruit was secretly sold at different prices for those who could pay immediately and those who might pay later. He consoles himself by saying that this was necessary to enable him to bring up his eight children, but like a thorn embedded in the body, these regrets continue to prick: "When it comes to business, you can't earn anything without telling lies. It was only by living with such ruses that I managed to raise eight children, educate them all, and buy them whatever they needed."

But if Ayya does not hold himself to the strictest standards of honesty in transactions, he is astonishingly without bitterness about events or people that robbed him of everything—his close friend in Burma to whom he entrusted his shop when his brother and he left with just two trunks as the war broke out, but for which he never recovered any compensation; the man who ran away with one of these trunks on the long march through the forest in Burma; or even perhaps the father-in-law who so humiliated him as to make him bathe and clean the buffalo in his stall though he was the son-in-law and an assistant at his cloth shop.

There is also a disquiet that stays with him for actions over which he could have had little or no control. For instance, he repeatedly returns to the haunting story of a man, a fellow villager whom they were forced to abandon during their treacherous trek through the Burmese jungle as they escaped escalating ethnic violence. Yet they could have hardly survived if they had stopped to share the meager supplies of water with everyone who needed it, or stopped to offer succor to those who were unable to continue and succumbing to cholera or other diseases.

Stories of heroic acts, of overcoming formidable obstacles, and of great solidarities forged during disasters are often laced in human life with the stories of betrayal that haunt survivors. In Ayya's case it is the juxtaposition of contradictory affects in registering death and loss that is striking: stoic indifference and inability to register grief at the deaths of intimate female relatives, on one side, and enduring sorrow on having touched the limits of the human in the act of abandonment, on the other side. He is never simply *this* or *that*—the man who is overcome with a painful inexpressivity in the face of the most intimate deaths is the same man whose conscience is haunted by the betrayals that many others might have simply seen as the inevitable cost of one's survival in such circumstances.

The vocabulary of the bazaar then indicates much more than a form of representation. Anand suggests that it reflects Ayya's mode of being, the practices through which a moral self is created and sustained. This thought touches on a profound idea that I have myself encountered in Sanskrit texts and in people's lives: that man is born in debt to ancestors, to the earth, to death itself. In Ayya's rendering he does not want to leave the world indebted to anyone. When talking of giving and taking, he says at one point that this happens not only in the market but also in the family. Now contemplating his death he says, "Dying in America would make for a very expensive burial. And it wouldn't be possible to bring my body back here either. This is why I won't be going back to America any more. From now on I will remain in India."

Not that Ayya has any doubts about the filial piety of his two highly successful sons and son-in-law who live in America, but a lifetime of frugality has impressed itself on his body and become his disposition. Yet can one leave life without a single debt? I found it particularly moving that it is in the company of the son who has inherited the shop, perhaps less brilliant in worldly terms, and the daughter-in-law with whom he lives in Madurai that he finds the ability to accept that if man is born in debt then perhaps he dies in some debt, too.

Describing how his daughter-in-law lovingly put ointment on his sores after surgery for oral cancer, or how she cooked soft food without much spice so that he could eat and regain his strength, he says, "My daughter-in-law Nirmala—she is the only reason that I have lived until the age of ninety-four. It's Nirmala that keeps me alive day by day." By acknowledging the debt to Nirmala for keeping him alive, and by planning with such care his eventual death so that his children in America are not encumbered with the cost of his burial, Ayya embodies what it means to be attracted to a life of frugality—turning compulsion into a willing acceptance of the fate of who one is and who one has become.

What kind of inheritance does Anand Pandian, the grandson and anthropologist, receive in this act of writing? First, one must be attentive to the enormous efforts his parents and uncles and aunts must have made to keep their parents and his grandparents alive to him and to others of his generation. Thus, though the story unfolds as a dialogue between grandfather and grandson, there is the loving labor of the other generations woven into the texture of this life.

Ayya claims in one place that Anand's parents were not very open to taking him out to the park. He says, "I was the first one to show Anand the light of the sun—though he was still very young, he found this delightful." One scene of inheritance in anthropology might be for each generation to vanquish its ancestors in order to find its autonomy. But another might be to ask "how did I learn to delight in the light of the sun?" The picture of originality and innovation that privileges the rejection of the past might then be replaced by another picture: learning to recover the joys of one's first encounters with the world through the eyes of the elders whose questions we inherit, and also recovering the joy we give them in making their questions our own. As Anand says, "Ayya and I have been doing a lot of digging, especially in the last couple of years, seeking to uncover such forgotten remains from buried times. In trying to make sense of what we've found, I've also had to look more closely beneath my own feet, back to the soil in which they too were planted."

In the complex working out of his inheritance, Anand traverses many questions. Does he take pride in being a Nadar as one of his uncles asks him? How does he negotiate the slight feeling of nausea that seems to overcome him on occasion as he sees everything being converted by Ayya into a question of profit and loss? Does Anand go back to the questions he asked Ayya and wonder what would have happened if he had been able to open a pathway to talk about the loss of Rupavathi, Ayya's daughter and the aunt he never got to know?

How is it that the difficulty Ayya has with talking of his sisters and his daughter finds an echo in Anand's own enshrining of men and boys as the proper inheritors of Ayya's legacy? He writes, "The truth of this story was etched with startling clarity, most especially, on the bodies of the men and boys gathered in those rooms." But the truth of the story also lies with those other figures—mothers, sisters, daughters—whose spectral presence and actual absence equally define the story of how men come to claim their masculinity in the world of kinship and in the world of knowledge-making.

We as readers cannot know what questions continue to haunt Anand about his grandfather's life and his own collaboration in remaking it as a text. But we are privileged to share the remarkable dream that he recounts, which tells Anand Pandian the anthropologist that his own work is like the retracing of marks that Ayya has left on him. For all his frugality, Ayya does sometimes indulge in stray thoughts that his life could have been different. He could have stayed on in Burma, like one of his uncles did, speaking the local languages; and he could have married a Burmese girl and lived a different kind of life. Perhaps the grandson has found his own vocation in this unrealized fleeting dream. Perhaps originality, in our work, lies in being able to retrace the steps taken or imagined by those who went before us, and in creating pathways for those who will follow us by sharing our stories with them.

Although there are no guarantees that we will know how to inherit our past, the remarkable fact that we sometimes do find connections with our ancestors and elders is reward enough. If Ayya reads this afterword, he might think of this itself as a bargain with time.

# ACKNOWLEDGMENTS

This book itself is a work of acknowledgment, recording debts impossible to repay. I am grateful to all those who have lent it shape and texture through their stories and counsel. My aunts, uncles, cousins, and other relatives have been patient with my questions—I hope they will forgive me for the unexpected directions that their words may have taken here. This book could not have happened without the home in Anna Nagar that Senthi Chithappa and Nimmi Chithi have made for Ayya, for me, and for so many of our conversations over so many years. Muruga Chithappa, Meena Athai and Kanna Chithappa have also been essential guides.

This book also has a foothold in anthropology, and I am thankful to all my teachers, both formal and informal, for their lessons. In particular, I would like to thank M. S. S. Pandian for introducing me many years ago to the social history of the Nadar caste and Lawrence Cohen for his sensitivity to being a grandson. Thanks to my colleagues at Johns Hopkins University, I know of no place more congenial to anthropological inquiry than this one. I am especially grateful to Jane Guyer, Clara Han, and Naveeda Khan, and to Veena Das, whose generous afterword here offers only the slightest hint of how deeply she has nurtured this project. I am also grateful to many students at Johns Hopkins for their enthusiasm for this project: Bridget Kustin, David Platzer, and Megha Sehdev in particular, and most especially Andrew Brandel and Ryan Kirlin for their incisive readings of the whole manuscript.

Novelist Su. Venkatesan wrote an extraordinary foreword for the original Tamil edition of this book, through which I came to see, for the first time, so much of what was at stake in this project and in my anthropological work more generally. He introduced me to the other central figure in that Tamil edition, writer Kamalalayan, without whom that book would not have found its body. I have learned enormously from the many thoughtful responses and reviews that the Tamil edition has provoked, most especially from my dialogues with two reporters from *The Hindu,* B. Kolappan and D. Karthikeyan. I remain deeply indebted to all the elder men and women of Tamil Nadu who have shared stories of their lives over the last fifteen years; though they may not appear here by name, their lessons suffuse each turn of this story.

I want to express my gratitude and deepest respect for Kalachuvadu publisher Kannan, who first saw in this project a book worth publishing. Rebecca Tolen at Indiana University Press has been enthusiastic and supportive from the first of our conversations about Ayya's story, and I am grateful to her for making a home for this story in English. I am also grateful to the Indiana University Press staff. Two external reviewers shared challenging readings of a draft manuscript, as did Urmila Dasgupta, giving me a glimpse of many unseen dimensions of its potential. In particular, I am thankful for the extraordinary reading made by Robert Desjarlais, who, more than anyone else, helped me to see its anthropological orientation. And Michael Jackson has also been a tremendous source of inspiration, and indeed, hope.

Throughout the many years in which this project slowly took shape, my mother, Lalitha Pandian, and my father, M. Ganesa Pandian, have been an unstinting well of recollections, advice, and support. My father has been a fellow traveler all along, taking Ayya and me to Burma in 2002 and reading countless drafts and missives concerning his father's life in the years that followed. My grandfather M. Soundraraj read the entire manuscript, as did my parents-in-law, Devika and K. B. Nair, and my brother-in-law Prasanth Manthena; I am grateful for their stories and reflections. I am indebted to my brother Karthik for his continuous counsel and to my sister Vidhya for reading these stories aloud with her children.

Sanchita Balachandran has been a tireless sounding board throughout this project and has read innumerable versions of every page with profound and sometimes fearsome insight. I am grateful to our son, Karun, for asking so casually one evening if I knew Ayya's father, prompting me to marvel that in fact I did, because of this book that Ayya and I had been writing together. Our daughter, Uma, was born just as I was finishing this book, and I have her to thank for the peculiar clarity that comes with sleepless and wonderstruck nights.

And then there's Ayya, who took me first, as he says, into the sunlight. I'm thankful for the chance to have walked along beside him.

~

My story—my autobiography, my life history—has been written here in an expansive form, and in great detail. I hope readers have found it enjoyable and interesting.

However, I would also like this book to record, to some small extent, the story of the eldest son of my eldest son: Anand Pandian, the thirty-nine-year-old writer of this story, and a master of all the world's arts. I will tell you some of what I know about his unfinished history. I hope that you will read this too with interest.

Although Anand Pandian was born in America, I have seen and spent time with him on many occasions. There were many times, when he was in India, that I worried about his health.

He has traveled to forty countries around the world and learned about the lives of people in those places. Sleeping on the silty earth of India's villages, he has asked about life there and listened to the songs of elderly women. In the village of Karunakkamuthanpatti, he stayed in the house of a poor farmer, helped his family, and ate with them. He has shared small glasses of tea with people of all castes, in a spirit of equality.

He stayed in the Cumbum Taluka to complete his research, mingling with the people of those villages, talking with them, and eating what they shared in friendship. He helped those who needed help. When he completed his research, he provided a feast for the villagers and went reluctantly back to America. He is working there as an associate professor at the renowned Johns Hopkins University. Whenever he has free time, he writes books for college students to read. He has toiled without a break for twelve hours each day to write and complete this book.

His wife's name is Sanchita. Like him, she is very skillful with her work.

They have one son, about whom I know a lot as well. His name is Karun. He is four years old. He is growing up to be someone ten times as wise as all of us, his father, mother, grandfather, grandmother, and me.

Readers, please also note this. Anand has come 22,000 kilometers from America to meet and speak with me and with many other writers, and he deserves my gratitude for having struggled this much to finish and publish this book.

I hope that all of you reading this book will find some happiness.

*Vanakkam.*

M. P. Mariappan
January 15, 2012
Madurai

# NOTES

### 1. A Century of Experience

1. *Paati* is grandmother in Tamil. *Ayya* literally means father but is used more widely as an honorific.

2. With a population of 1.5 million, Madurai is the third-largest city in India's southernmost state of Tamil Nadu.

### 2. In Some Village, Somewhere

1. To the east of India, across the Bay of Bengal, Burma was annexed to British India in the nineteenth century.

2. Literally, "nose-woman" and "ear-woman."

3. Late medieval Tamil moral texts in verse, widely taught in traditional veranda schools.

### 4. Things I Didn't Know I'd Lost

1. A flowering tree with edible seedpods, sometimes known in English as Manila tamarind.

2. *Vedar,* meaning "hunter" in Tamil, is a term associated with the unruly margins of settled villages and their customary denizens.

### 6. A Decade in Burma

1. A wealthy Tamil mercantile caste associated with banking and moneylending operations.

2. Until 1957, sixteen annas equaled one Indian rupee.

### 8. When the War Came

1. At least two hundred people were killed and over a thousand others injured as Burmese crowds and gangs attacked Indian mosques, shops, and homes in many towns and villages throughout lowland Burma in 1938.

2. *Kala* is a derogatory term for dark-skinned foreigners, especially those of Indian origin.

3. South Indian dumplings and crepes made from a fermented batter of rice and black gram.

### 10. A New Life at Home

1. *Pettai*s were peripheral market compounds organized by Nadar merchants in southern Tamil Nadu.

2. The Tamil version of Kokkoka's medieval Sanskrit *Ratirahasya* on the secrets of love.

3. In Dravidian kinship terminology, *mama* is one's father-in-law, mother's brother, or father's sister's husband.

4. A savory snack made of gram flour.

### 12. Dealing Cloth in a Time of War

1. The zamindari system of landlordship was one of two principal arrangements of land tenure in colonial India.

### 14. A Foothold in Madurai

1. A *veshti* is a single long piece of cloth wrapped by men around the waist.

2. Seed of the areca palm, betel nut is commonly chewed as a stimulant in India.

### 16. A Shop of My Own

1. Localities in the south Indian states of Tamil Nadu and Kerala.

2. From 1957 onward, 100 *paisa* equaled one Indian rupee.

### 18. Branches in Many Directions

1. The Indo-Chinese Himalayan border war of 1962.

### 20. Between Madurai and America

1. A *lungi* is a loop of cloth worn by men around the waist.

### 22. What Comes Will Come

1. E. V. Ramasamy, known as Periyar, founder of the rationalist Self-Respect Movement in the early twentieth century.

2. In prayer to Sakthi, a name for the Brahmanical Hindu goddess and consort of Shiva.

### 24. Burma, Once Again

1. The opening of Ayya's six-page written record of our Burma trip, the only diary pages I have known him to keep.

### 26. Giving and Taking

1. *Patru* in Tamil, means not only "debt" but also "relationship" and "devotion."

# BIBLIOGRAPHY

Adas, Michael. *The Burma Delta: Economic Development and Social Change on an Asian Rice Frontier, 1852–1941.* Madison: University of Wisconsin Press, 1974.

Amin, Shahid. "Gandhi as Mahatma: Gorakhpur District, Eastern UP, 1921–2." In *Selected Subaltern Studies,* edited by Ranajit Guha and Gayatri Chakravorty Spivak. New York: Oxford University Press, 1988. 288–350.

Appadurai, Arjun. *Modernity at Large: Cultural Dimensions of Globalization.* Minneapolis: University of Minnesota Press, 1996.

Arnold, David, and Stuart Blackburn. *Telling Lives in India: Biography, Autobiography, and Life History.* Bloomington: Indiana University Press, 2004.

Bate, Bernard. *Tamil Oratory and the Dravidian Aesthetic: Democratic Practice in South India.* New York: Columbia University Press, 2009.

Bayly, Susan. *Caste, Society, and Politics in India from the Eighteenth Century to the Modern Age.* Cambridge: Cambridge University Press, 1999.

Benjamin, Walter. "The Storyteller: Observations on the Works of Nikolai Leskov." In *Illuminations.* New York: Schocken Books, 1968. 83–108.

Bloch, Ernst. *The Principle of Hope.* Cambridge, Mass.: MIT Press, 1986.

Boo, Katherine. *Behind the Beautiful Forevers: Life, Death and Hope in a Mumbai Undercity.* New York: Random House, 2012.

Brown, Judith M. *Global South Asians: Introducing the Modern Diaspora.* Cambridge: Cambridge University Press, 2006.

Chakrabarty, Dipesh. *Provincializing Europe: Postcolonial Thought and Historical Difference.* Princeton: Princeton University Press, 2000.

Chari, Sharad. *Fraternal Capital: Peasant-Workers, Self-Made Men, and Globalization in Provincial India.* Stanford: Stanford University Press, 2004.

Chatterjee, Partha. *The Nation and Its Fragments.* New Delhi: Oxford University Press, 1994.

Cohen, Lawrence. *No Aging in India: Alzheimer's, the Bad Family, and Other Modern Things.* Berkeley: University of California Press, 1998.

Crapanzano, Vincent. *Imaginative Horizons: An Essay in Literary-Philosophical Anthropology.* Chicago: University of Chicago Press, 2004.

Daniel, E. Valentine. *Fluid Signs: Being a Person the Tamil Way*. Berkeley: University of California Press, 1984.

Das, Veena. *Life and Words: Violence and the Descent into the Ordinary*. Berkeley: University of California Press, 2006.

Das, Veena, and Ranendra Das. *Sociology and Anthropology of Economic Life I: The Moral Embedding of Economic Action*. New Delhi: Oxford University Press, 2010.

Deb, Siddharth. *The Beautiful and the Damned: A Portrait of the New India*. New York: Faber and Faber, 2011.

Desjarlais, Robert. *Sensory Biographies: Lives and Deaths among Nepal's Yolmo Buddhists*. Berkeley: University of California Press, 2003.

Dube, Saurabh, and Ishita Banerjee-Dube. *Modern Makeovers: Oxford Handbook of Modernity in South Asia*. New Delhi: Oxford University Press, 2011.

Freeman, James. *Untouchable: An Indian Life History*. London: George Allen and Unwin, 1979.

Gadgil, Madhav, and Ramachandra Guha. *Ecology and Equity: The Use and Abuse of Nature in Contemporary India*. New York: Routledge Press, 1995.

Ghosh, Amitav. *The Glass Palace*. New York: Random House, 2000.

Gidwani, Vinay, and K. Sivaramakrishnan. "Circular Migration and Rural Cosmopolitanism in India." *Contributions to Indian Sociology* 37, nos. 1–2 (2003): 339–67.

Graeber, David. *Debt: The First 5,000 Years*. New York: Melville House, 2011.

Gupta, Akhil. *Postcolonial Developments: Agriculture in the Making of Modern India*. Durham: Duke University Press, 2008.

Guyer, Jane. *Marginal Gains: Monetary Transactions in Central Africa*. Chicago: University of Chicago Press, 2004.

Han, Clara. *Life in Debt: Times of Care and Violence in Neoliberal Chile*. Berkeley: University of California Press, 2012.

Hann, Chris, and Keith Hart. *Market and Society: The Great Transformation Today*. Cambridge: Cambridge University Press, 2009.

Hardgrave, Robert L. *The Nadars of Tamilnad: The Political Culture of a Community in Change*. Berkeley: University of California Press, 1969.

Jackson, Michael. *Life Within Limits: Well-Being in a World of Want*. Durham: Duke University Press, 2011.

Jesudasan, Hephzibah. *Ma Nee*. Madras, India: Christian Literature Society, 1989.

Kapur, Akash. *India Becoming: A Portrait of Life in Modern India*. New York: Riverhead, 2012.

Kulke, Hermann, K. Kesavapany, and Vijay Sakhuja, eds. *Nagapattinam to Suvarnadwipa: Reflections on the Chola Naval Expeditions to Southeast Asia*. Singapore: Institute of Southeast Asian Studies, 2009.

Laidlaw, James. *Riches and Renunciation: Religion, Economy, and Society among the Jains*. New York: Oxford University Press, 1995.

Lamb, Sarah. *Aging and the Indian Diaspora: Cosmopolitan Families in India and Abroad.* Bloomington: Indiana University Press, 2009.

———. *White Saris and Sweet Mangoes: Aging, Gender, and the Body in North India.* Berkeley: University of California Press, 2000.

Liechty, Mark. *Suitably Modern: Making Middle-Class Culture in a New Consumer Society.* Princeton: Princeton University Press, 2002.

Mariappan, M. P., and Anand Pandian. *Mitcham Meethi, Oru Anubava Kanakku.* Nagercoil: Kalachuvadu Publications, 2012.

Marriott, McKim. "Hindu Transactions: Diversity without Dualism." In *Transaction and Meaning: Directions in the Anthropology of Exchange and Symbolic Behavior,* edited by Bruce Kapferer. Philadelphia: Institute for the Study of Human Issues, 1976. 109–42.

Mazzarella, William. *Shoveling Smoke: Advertising and Globalization in Contemporary India.* Durham: Duke University Press, 2003.

Mines, Mattison. *Public Faces, Private Voices: Community and Individuality in South India.* Delhi: Oxford University Press, 1996.

Miyazaki, Hirokazu. *The Method of Hope: Anthropology, Philosophy, and Fijian Knowledge.* Stanford: Stanford University Press, 2004.

Narayan, Kirin. *My Family and Other Saints.* Chicago: University of Chicago Press, 2007.

Nehru, Jawaharlal. *The Discovery of India.* London: Meridian Books, 1956.

Pandian, Anand. *Crooked Stalks: Cultivating Virtue in South India.* Durham: Duke University Press, 2009.

Pandian, Anand, and Daud Ali. *Ethical Life in South Asia.* Bloomington: Indiana University Press, 2010.

Pandian, M. S. S. *Brahmin and Non-Brahmin.* New Delhi: Permanent Black, 2006.

Parry, Jonathan, and Maurice Bloch. *Money and the Morality of Exchange.* Cambridge: Cambridge University Press, 1989.

Pinney, Christopher. *Camera Indica.* Chicago: University of Chicago Press, 1997.

Poovey, Mary. *A History of the Modern Fact: Problems of Knowledge in the Sciences of Wealth and Society.* Chicago: University of Chicago Press, 1998.

Quigley, Declan. *The Interpretation of Caste.* Oxford: Clarendon Press, 1993.

Racine, Josiane, and Jean-Luc Racine. *Viramma: Life of an Untouchable.* New York: Verso, 1997.

Rudner, David. *Caste and Capitalism in Colonial India: The Nattukottai Chettiars.* Berkeley: University of California Press, 1994.

Rukmani, R. "Urbanisation and Socio-Economic Change in Tamil Nadu, 1901–91." *Economic and Political Weekly* 29, nos. 51–52 (1994): 3263–72.

*Statistical Abstract Relating to British India from 1910–11 to 1919–20.* London: His Majesty's Stationery Office, 1922.

Tinker, Hugh. "A Forgotten Long March: The Indian Exodus from Burma, 1942." *Journal of Southeast Asian Studies* 6, no. (1975): 1–15.

———. "Indians in South East Asia: Imperial Auxiliaries." In *South Asians Overseas: Migration and Ethnicity,* edited by Colin Clarke et. al. Cambridge: Cambridge University Press, 1990. 39–56.

Trawick, Margaret. *Notes on Love in a Tamil Family.* Berkeley: University of California Press, 1990.

Trivedi, Lisa N. "Visually Mapping the 'Nation': Swadeshi Politics in Nationalist India, 1920–1930." *Journal of Asian Studies* 62, no. 1 (2003): 11–41.

Vairamuthu. *Kallikattu Ithikasam.* Chennai, India: Surya Literature Limited, 2001.

ANAND PANDIAN is an associate professor of anthropology at Johns Hopkins University.

M. P. MARIAPPAN is a retired fruit merchant living in the south Indian city of Madurai.

VEENA DAS is Krieger-Eisenhower Professor of Anthropology at Johns Hopkins University.

CPSIA information can be obtained at www.ICGtesting.com
Printed in the USA
LVOW01s1909080414

380845LV00020B/81/P